AWAKEN

Inside Yoga Meditation
A Complete Guide

AWAKEN

Inside Yoga Meditation
A Complete Guide

REVEREND JAGANATH CARRERA

Yoga Life Publications

Woodland Park, New Jersey

Copyright © 2012 Jaganath Carrera
All rights reserved, including the right to reproduce this book
or any portions thereof in any form.

Printed in the United States of America

First Printing

Library of Congress Control Number: 2012935618

ISBN: 978-0-692-01730-2

Cover design by Domenick Lorelli and Catherine Callari
of Lorelli Associates, NYC, NY

Layout by Kemper Conwell of Pixels, Charlottesville, Virginia

Yoga Life Publications
Yoga Life Society
Woodland Park, New Jersey 07424
www.yogalifesociety.com

When you go to bed at night, stillness leads to sleep.
When you meditate, stillness leads to awakening.

CONTENTS

Dedication x
Acknowledgements xi
Prologue: This is Meditation xii
Preface xiii

What's in This Book xv

Is Meditation for Me? 1
    Frequently Asked Questions 2
    Why People Meditate 4
    Quick Start Guide 8

How to Meditate 11
    Yoga Meditation: A Five Thousand Year Tradition 12
    The Technique 15
    Objects for Meditation 20
    Visualization 22
    Sound 25
    Prayer 34
    Self-Inquiry 35
    Body Centered Meditation 37
    How To Combine Techniques 39

Building Blocks for Success in Meditation 41
    Where to Meditate 42
    How You Sit Makes a Difference 44
    Breathing Practices 47
    Affirmations, Chants, Prayers 52
    The Golden Moment 53
    How to End a Session 55
    Develop a Sensible Practice 56

The Distracted Mind Syndrome 61
    What Happens When the Mind Shakes 62
    More Obstacles 68
    Experiences in Meditation 72

Sample Meditation Routines 75
   Routine One: A Solid Foundation 76
   Routine Two: Drop Your Burdens 79

Success is in the Details: Hints and Suggestions That Work 83
   Regularity 84
   The Essential Triad: Intention, Attention,
      Nonjudgemental Attitude 87
   Meditation in Action: Karma Yoga,
      The Science of Actions and Their Consequences 91
   Diet: What's On Your Plate and What's In Your Mind
      are Related 98
   Meditation Journal: A Way to Track Your Progress 102
   Hatha Yoga and Meditation 104
   Mindful Living: Awaken to Life 106
   Qualities of Successful Meditators 109

Samadhi: Meditation's Finish Line 117
   Absorption, Insight, Wisdom 118
   Samadhi in the Yoga Sutras of Patanjali 120
   The Four States of Awareness 123

The Roots of Yoga Meditation 125
   Traditional Texts That Speak on Meditation 126
   Yoga Sutras of Patanjali 127
   Bhagavad Gita 139
   Hatha Yoga Pradeepika 143
   Upanishads 145
   Yoga and Religion 147
   Is a Guru Necessary? 151

Explore More 159
   The Three Faculties of Mind: Manas, Buddhi, Ahamkara 160
   The Root of All Obstacles 162
   Stillness Redefined 164
   Yoga and Emotions 167
   Meditation and the Brain: A Little Science 168

Epilogue: Awaken Inside Yoga Meditation 171
Sanskrit Glossary 172
English Glossary 191

For Further Study 195
About Reverend Jaganath Carrera 197
About the Yoga Life Society and Yoga Life Publications 198

DEDICATION

To my master, Sri Swami Satchidananda Maharaj, an embodiment of the highest attainment of meditation.

To the great masters of all traditions who have freely passed on their insights into meditation, the nature of the mind, and of life.

To all students of Yoga who strive to fulfill their potential for Self-realization.

To all those who seek peace, joy, love, and meaning in life.

ACKNOWLEDGEMENTS

Books are rarely the product of one person's efforts. That's certainly true here. I am grateful to all those who have contributed to making this text possible.

My Gurudev, Sri Swami Satchidananda Maharaj. He is the soul and inspiration behind the teachings presented here. His words and guidance are never-ending fountains of wisdom.

Reverend Janaki Carrera, my wife. She's been on the front lines of this project for two years, reading drafts, listening to my ideas, and giving me unfailingly sage advice.

Marcie Amba Wallace, who edited the final text, making it presentable to the public.

Kemper Conwell of Pixels in Charlottesville, Virginia, whose expertise in layout made the information clear, attractive, and accessible.

Domenick Lorelli and Catherine Callari of Lorelli Associates, who graciously donated their time and talents in designing the beautful and evocative cover of this book.

Thank you all for helping make this project possible.

PROLOGUE
This is Meditation

In the soft, early morning light, your meditation space looks welcoming and secure. Over the past few months it has transformed into an island of quiet refuge in your busy life. As you gently close your eyes, you cherish the time that you take for yourself. It is a time of retreat that reconnects you to a place within that nurtures you throughout the day. When you arise, you are ready to face a day that is filled with infinite opportunities.

Meditation has become a vital part of your daily life, not just because it relaxes you or improves your ability to focus your attention. You have discovered the deeper part of you – your heart and essence. At that level there is no stress, fear, or strife. Meditation has helped you become more aware of the unshakable peace that is your True Nature. You have no doubt of meditation's transforming power because you have experienced it.

PREFACE

Arise! Awake! Follow the teachings of the great ones and realize your True Nature, the Self.
Katha Upanishad

Awaken

Look again at the above quote. Are the first two words out of order? Are we being urged to arise before we awake? Why this reversal of actions?

To awaken is a good thing. It's really the best thing that can happen to you. It means to be fully alive, rooted in the moment, and free from the conceptions, misperceptions, fears, and anxieties that obscure the peace of your True Nature. It is Self-realization, enlightenment, nirvana, and happiness beyond words. It is your birthright.

Arise comes first because we need to do something to awaken. It won't come by itself. This is where meditation comes in. It dissolves ingrained thought-habits that cloud awareness and obscure the experience of our True Nature.

Until we awaken from false and limited notions of who we are, we will never really know peace, never know the joys of unconditional love, and never unearth our deepest purpose for being.

Inside Yoga Meditation

It's not uncommon for Yoga students to consider Yoga and meditation to be two different practices. Perhaps this misperception stems from using the word Yoga in a limited way, referring only to Hatha Yoga, the physical branch of Yoga. In fact, meditation theory and practice has been an integral part of Yoga since its inception.

Yoga is holistic. Examine the following list and note how each branch of Yoga addresses an essential facet of what defines us as human beings. Each path includes teachings, traditions, and practices designed to develop that quality to its highest. Taken together, these branches bring about a complete and harmonious development of the individual.

- **Jnana Yoga:** refines the discriminative capacity of the mind through study, discernment, and self-analysis.

- **Karma Yoga:** selfless service addresses interactions with others in a way that reduces selfish motivations.
- **Bhakti Yoga:** devotion to a name and form of God opens the heart and makes use of the inborn inclination to devote oneself to a cause or someone to create a greater, more fulfilling reality.
- **Japa Yoga:** repetition of mantras that access deep, pre-language aspects of our being and that connect us to the Higher Self.
- **Raja Yoga:** the science of the mind and Self, uses the will and is based on moral and ethical precepts.
- **Hatha Yoga:** includes postures, breathing practices, and deep relaxation techniques to bring balance, strength, and suppleness to the body.

The history of Yoga is even more varied than the list suggests. Yoga has evolved with influences from other spiritual traditions and philosophies, prominent teachers, and from the times and places it is practiced. It is not a monolithic, one-size-fits-all science. Some traditions, modern and ancient, may emphasize one branch over the others. Many, as in this book, teach an integral approach, a synthesis of all the branches of Yoga practiced according to one's temperament.

The theories behind the different schools of Yoga may also differ. For example, some philosophies teach that consciousness and matter are two expressions of one reality; others that consciousness and matter are eternal, but separate realities. Some worship a personal God, some do not. Regardless of these differences, all schools of Yoga (including Hatha Yoga) include some form of meditation or meditative practice at its core.

WHAT'S IN THIS BOOK

There are nine sections; six are on meditation theory and practice. The last three explore some of the wisdom texts of Yoga and a few scientific insights into meditation.

Is Meditation for Me begins with frequently asked questions. It covers the definition of meditation, its principal benefits, and how it fits into spiritual life. Next, you'll find a *Quick Start Guide* should you wish to get a taste of meditation today. The *Quick Start Guide* also serves as an outline for reviewing the basics of meditation.

How to Meditate presents meditation theory and techniques.

Building Blocks for Success in Meditation introduces the major elements of a meditation session. This is followed by suggestions for cultivating a practice that works and is suited to your taste and temperament.

The Distracted Mind Syndrome reviews the obstacles that meditators face and the prescription for overcoming them. Also included are signs of progress in meditation.

Sample Meditation Routines contains two routines you can use as is, or as guides for developing your own practice.

Success is in the Details: Hints and Suggestions That Work contains suggestions for how to make meditation a part of your daily life. You'll find the best of the best in hints. Each is a tried and true gem that can boost your practice.

Samadhi: Meditation's Finish Line explores the ultimate goal of meditation, the transformative experience that brings unshakable peace and joy. The technical term is *samadhi*, absorption, or superconscious state.

The Roots of Yoga Meditation is an introduction to several of the primary texts for the tradition of meditation in Yoga.

Explore More takes you further into the theory of meditation and the mind. Included is an introduction to a few recent scientific discoveries regarding meditation.

Glossaries. There are two: a Sanskrit Glossary and an English Glossary for pertinent terms used in this book. Some terms have an expanded definition that should supplement further study in meditation and Yoga.

Reference Notes

This book is a little bit like a non-alphabetical encyclopedia. It is designed to be a reference for continued study as well as a manual of basic theory and instruction. To keep each topic complete, some key principles and practices are found in more than one section, usually with different supporting information.

Footnotes. This little book has a good number of footnotes. Don't be intimidated by them. They are meant to expand on the text and provide a way to cross reference information for deeper understanding and study.

Scriptural references. Several classic texts on Yoga are referenced in this book, with the Yoga Sutras of Patanjali and the Bhagavad Gita being the most prominent. The words Sutra or sutras always refers to Patanjali's work. Gita refers to the Bhagavad Gita. The numbers that appear after the quotes refer to the chapter and verse in the text.

Sanskrit transliteration and translation. We have decided not to use one of the standard methods for the transliteration of Sanskrit terms. Instead, we have used a simplified system meant to make reading the text more fluid. Also, while it is not strictly grammatically correct to add "s" to pluralize Sanskrit words, we have done so for certain key terms since it is in keeping with the trend of anglicizing Sanskrit. For example, it is now common to add an "s" to asana and mantra to indicate their plural.

Sanskrit terms are italicized when they are first translated.

A note on personal instruction. If you are looking to meditation to relieve stress, and improve concentration, you'll probably do fine without a teacher. However, if your objective is to allow meditation to take you to the outer reaches of the mind, to experience a transcendent state beyond relativities, a seasoned instructor is invaluable.

IS MEDITATION FOR ME?

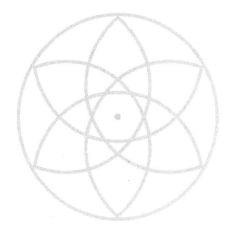

FREQUENTLY ASKED QUESTIONS

Who is meditation for?

Anyone who would like to experience greater peace, wellbeing, improved mental clarity, and meaning in life. It is also great for regulating blood pressure and for reducing the symptoms that result from stress related disorders.

Are the techniques of meditation difficult to learn?

No.

Are they difficult to master?

It does take some time and practice, but not stressful, grueling efforts. To attain the greatest benefits from meditation, you do need to sit regularly. It's like any other skill. The more you do it, the better you get at it. Know one thing for certain: meditation can be enjoyable and rewarding beyond any expectations.

Is meditation a practice that is best suited for intellectuals?

No. Success in meditation does not depend on knowing lots of theory or the ability to dissect and inspect fine points of philosophy. Sometimes this can even get in the way. Meditation is not thinking. It is learning how to make the mind come to an alert, focused, restful state of awareness.

It might be encouraging to know that you've probably already experienced meditative states. Haven't you been so absorbed in a book or movie that you forgot where you were and lost track of time? With your attention focused, you felt that you lacked nothing. Problems and cares were left behind. It was a taste of meditation.

Most people stumble into such states from time to time. By making meditation a regular part of life, we learn to create that state of mind whenever we wish, carry it with us throughout the day, and bring it to even deeper, more satisfying levels.

Isn't meditation for those who are devoted to their religion and use it as a way to deepen faith?

Yes, but that's not the whole story. Meditation is not based on any particular faith. It is a science based on one principle: a mind that is peaceful, clear, and one-pointed will realize its innate potential to experience profound happiness.

Aren't there articles of faith that I need to follow? All I need to do is to learn the technique of meditation?

Meditation is not limited to any particular faith tradition, or any faith tradition at all. Agnostics and atheists can also enjoy its benefits. However, much of the language and many of the hints are of a "spiritual" nature. If you are not comfortable with words like God, Spirit, or Divine, you can substitute other words. Terms such as Being, Pure Consciousness, the Way, and Reality are just as valid.

All words and concepts – spiritual or not – are inadequate ways of describing the indescribable: the essence and source of existence. To stay away from the limiting and often misleading words used to describe it, sacred texts such as the *Upanishads* use *tat* (that) or *sat – chit – ananda* (existence, awareness, bliss). Both ways avoid using traditional names for God. This suggests that the ultimate reality is beyond simplistic labels, theory, and literal-minded sectarianism. It is known only through practice and direct experience. For example, sat – chit – ananda is the answer to three questions: Is there existence? (*Not, is there a God?*) What is its nature? How can the answers to the two previous questions affect me?

Isn't meditation based on Eastern philosophies like Buddhism and Hinduism?

Although this book references a number of Eastern teachings in general, and yogic teachings in particular, meditation is neither Eastern nor Western. It is a universal science that has been practiced for thousands of years all over the globe. While the particulars might differ, the essential technique is the same: in meditation, the mind learns how to attain an unbroken flow of attention towards a particular thought, image, or object. If we can maintain that flow for even a little while, we experience profound clarity and peace.

WHY PEOPLE MEDITATE

The practice of meditation has survived for thousands of years. What is it about meditation that makes it so long-lived?

Meditation speaks eloquently of the inborn impulse to find deep and lasting fulfillment. We look for something that can bring our anxieties, restlessness, questions, and insecurities to a satisfying resolution. When we've exhausted name, fame, possessions, and attainments in our search for happiness, we turn to the only place we may not have looked– within.

Let's look at some compelling reasons for practicing meditation.

Meditation is the Gateway to Self-realization

"Self" is a word used to designate our True Nature. It is that part of us that was never born, doesn't grow old or fall sick, and does not die. Free from strife and suffering, it is beyond the body and mind, but is the essence of both.

Why do we refer to the Self as our True Nature? We call it "true" because it does not change. It is outside the grasp of time. It is our "nature" because it is fundamental to us.

The Self is not an object to know. It is the knower, unbounded awareness, the changeless part of you that witnesses all. Yet, there are not many Selves, just one. Like the sun reflecting on countless drops of water, the Self is one and the same for all. We are like those droplets, never suspecting, or only vaguely aware, that we are not the image reflected on the surface, but the Sun itself. We *are* the Self.

Meditation is a Retreat

Meditation's benefits are realized not just from having attention focused on the object of meditation. The benefits are also derived from what we turn away from when we practice.

Meditation is a mini retreat. Accumulated stresses float away in the calm inner focus of meditation. We leave behind the cares that face our family, friends, and planet, and gain a fresh perspective on what's truly important. Also left behind are fears, anxieties, woes, successes, and failures.

We sit clear, still, and whole, content to simply be. In the act of meditation we find rare fulfillment and rest.

Is Meditation for Me?

Meditation Reduces Stress

Some thoughts cause stress, but not in meditation. Meditation teaches us that we don't need to stay away from certain thoughts to find peace – we need to change our relationship to them.

In meditation, thoughts are not experienced as fundamental to who we are, but as phenomena that pass *through* the mind. Thoughts are like storm clouds that move through the sky, but do not affect it. With continued practice, stressful thoughts gradually lose their influence over our moods and behavior even outside of meditation.

Meditation Brings Self-knowledge

Quieting the mind allows subconscious impressions to rise to conscious awareness. You'll be able to perceive hidden motives and thoughts. Over time, troublesome thought-habits, grumpiness, restlessness, and fears begin to vacate their comfy home in the dark corners of your mind. These nagging aspects of the mind have persisted because until now, you haven't perceived their origin and because you usually try to push them aside, considering them as nuisances or threats. Repression strengthens them, but if you can perceive and acknowledge them while maintaining a nonjudgmental attitude, you release them.

Meditation also reinforces existing virtues and uncovers ones you didn't know you had.

Meditation Strengthens the Mind's Ability to Probe and Discover

A focused mind naturally penetrates the object of its attention. This quality of mind makes meditation a powerful tool for attaining knowledge. If we look at most human accomplishments, we will find a mind that focused on an object or idea until it revealed its inner truths. In meditation, the mind is gradually brought to steady focus and dives to the heart of Nature, our problems, and the mind.

Meditation Leads to a Selfless State of Mind

We all would like to do good in this world, to leave it a little better than we found it. Meditation lifts us above matters of self-interest and leads to positive, selfless states of mind. Positive states of mind lead to positive, compassionate actions.

Meditation Brings You to the Golden Present

Meditation brings you into the present moment and helps keep you there even after meditating. The present moment contains not only problems we need to address, but the solutions to them. A focused mind is open to inner promptings and to creative solutions that often lie at the margins of our awareness.

A mind that rests in the present moment is without fear. Worry lives in the future. You dread what *may* come. Fear cannot survive in the present moment, which is the link to the Self and is outside of time. Fear dissolves as you gradually become rooted in the Self.

Meditation Opens the Way to Wisdom Through Right Relationship with the Ego

The ego is the sense of individuality. It is the feeling of being separate from all people and objects. While we *are* separate in body and mind, we are one in Spirit (pure consciousness). The ego masks this truth.

The nature of the ego is to consider itself as the center of the universe. Its primary focus is to navigate through life, avoiding pain while running after pleasure. Because its perspective is so narrow, anything that doesn't make sense to it, is dismissed as senseless. We miss so much when we are limited to the ego's point of view. Under the influence of the ego, understanding the deeper realities of life, self, and Self becomes a hopeless task.

In meditation, we focus our attention on something other than the ego's ceaseless inner promptings and rise to a new vantage point that opens the mind to truths it may have only imagined or glimpsed. Meditation dethrones the ego from the false perception that *it* is the center of the universe. A more global vision of life and self allows us to see the interconnectedness and harmony of all beings, objects, and events.

Meditation Helps You Discover Your True Worth

It's natural to spend a significant amount of time and energy looking for what is worthwhile in ourselves. We look to find traits, talents, and accomplishments that validate our worthiness.

Our greatest value is not based on attainments such as wealth, possessions, or success in business, relationships, sports, or politics.

While being a virtuous, giving person *is* meaningful and beneficial; our deepest worth lies more deeply within.

Realizing the Self is the ultimate reason we are here. Paradoxically, its attainment is not accomplished by *doing*, but by *being*. We could say that meditation is the science of learning to *cease doing*, and *begin being*. Pure being is existence, awareness, and peace.

Existence and truth are the same word in Sanskrit, *sat*. The ultimate truth is that we are born from, and live in, pure cosmic existence, but we can't rest in it until our minds become clear, peaceful and one-pointed. It is then that our individual awareness merges – experiences *yoga* – with the Self. Beyond any worldly accomplishments, it is this experience that validates who we are.

QUICK START GUIDE

This Quick Start Guide will guide you through the basic steps in a meditation session. It provides what you need to get started.

Though basic, the instructions are complete and provide a good review of the fundamentals. For this reason, it will also be useful for more experienced meditators.

This sample session should take about twenty minutes.

- Find a quiet spot where you won't likely be disturbed. Make sure that the space is not too cool, too warm, or stuffy.

- Sit comfortably cross-legged on the floor, on your heels, or on a chair.

- If you like, you can light a candle to help create a meditative mood.

- Make adjustments to your posture to ensure that you are comfortable. See that you are sitting upright, but not stiff. Shoulders are gently back and the chin parallel to the floor. The hands can be folded on the lap or resting palms up or down on the knees.

- Take five easy, deep, slow breaths through the nose. Keep your awareness focused on the entire duration of each inhalation and exhalation. Don't strain. Keeping the breathing rhythmic is more important than trying to force air into and out of the lungs. If you begin to feel a little lightheaded, stop and let the breathing return to normal.

- You can light some incense if you are not sensitive to smoke or fragrances (use incense made with natural ingredients). Find the right size stick. Ideally you shouldn't see smoke filling the room. There should only be a light, uplifting scent.

- Remind yourself not to be judgmental concerning the results. Resolve that you will create a space of lovingkindness[1] within yourself, a place of complete acceptance for whatever happens

---

[1] Lovingkindness is a term often used in Buddhism. To be loving is to be compassionate and to seek the welfare of others. To be kind is to put loving thoughts into action.

IS MEDITATION FOR ME?

during this meditation and of who you are. A safe, loving inner environment is key to success.

- Resolve that you will remain perfectly still once you begin focusing on the object of meditation.

- Affirm the reason you are meditating. For example, *I affirm that Peace is my True Nature, and to experience this, I will direct the flow of my attention toward my object of meditation.*

- Take a minute to simply watch the thoughts as they move through the mind. Don't try to control or affect them in any way. Just quietly observe them as they arise, develop, and fade away.

- Now turn your attention to the object of meditation. It can be anything you like and that you find uplifting. Good choices include mantras and breath awareness. You can repeat a mantra such as "OM *Shanti*" (OM Peace), or simply observe the flow of the breath.

    Meditation is a continuous flow of attention toward a thought or image. If you choose a mantra, mentally repeat it from beginning to the end of your session. Notice how it sounds. You can visualize the words as you repeat it, if you like. Keep the pace easy and moderate, neither too slow nor too quick.

    If you've chosen the breath, simply observe its natural flow into and out of the body. Don't try to regulate it in any way. Just watch the flow.

    Don't wrestle with or force the mind. That will only create tension and distractions.

- The attention will inevitably drift from the object of meditation. It even happens to seasoned practitioners, often many times during a single sitting. Your attention may wander off into chores for the day, pressing problems, bodily sensations, or outside distractions. Don't be concerned. This is a natural part of the process.

    Here's what to do: when the mind wanders, simply let go of the distracting thought. Ignore it and gently refocus on the object of meditation. Don't be concerned if you need to do this over and over. You don't need to have perfectly steady focus to experience many of the benefits of meditation.

Allow any anxiety over distracting thoughts to float away and dissolve into the gentle lovingkindness you have created within.

- Continue for fifteen minutes (a kitchen timer can be helpful). More advanced meditators may have longer sittings, but don't be concerned with that now. Fifteen minutes of even fairly shaky attention will work wonders...really.

- End the session by taking three deep, slow breaths through the nose.

- Sit for a minute or two just watching the mind as you did at the beginning of the session. Watch the thoughts as they arise, develop, and fade away. Notice how you feel.

- Repeat a prayer or affirmation for the peace and wellbeing of all beings.

- Get up, resolved to have a good day.

HOW TO MEDITATE

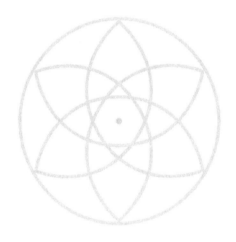

YOGA MEDITATION
A Five Thousand Year Tradition

Yoga: It's no longer associated with new-agers or children of the sixties. It's gone mainstream, at least parts of it.

Derived from the root, *yuj*, the word Yoga refers to the act of yoking or joining. Yuj is the root from which we derive the English word "yoke." Yoga can refer to the control of the senses, harnessing the power of a focused mind toward the attainment of enlightenment, or to the spiritual practices in general. In its highest sense, Yoga refers to the essential union of the individual with the Self. This union is experienced by a mind that is clear, calm, and focused.

Two authoritative texts on Yoga, the *Yoga Sutras of Patanjali*, and the B*hagavad Gita*, present these foundational definitions of Yoga:

> *The stilling of the modifications of the mindstuff is Yoga.* (1.2)
> Yoga Sutras

> E*quanimity of mind is Yoga.* (2.48)
> Bhagavad Gita

These definitions suggest that Yoga is not primarily a physical practice. Anything that brings the mind to a clear, tranquil state is a yogic practice.

Why the emphasis on steadiness of mind? Perception, habit, and motivation play a pivotal role in determining experiences of happiness and suffering.

A mind with scattered attention lacks self-knowledge, experiences much of life through preconceived notions, is prone to jumping to conclusions, and fails to perceive subtle implications of actions and events. A mind with focused, unclouded attention gains self-knowledge, operates with greater rationality and insight, and more accurately perceives the consequences of actions and occurrences. Most importantly, a mind that has attained such a state dissolves ignorance, the source of suffering. We awaken to our True Self.

The central role that the mind plays in Yoga can be summarized as:
- The ultimate goal of all people is to be happy.
- Peace and happiness is within us as our True Nature.

- Ignorance of our True Nature is the cause of all suffering.
- Ignorance is overcome, and the happiness we seek is attained, when the mind attains focus, clarity, and stillness.

The Ultimate Goal of All People is to be Happy

Every effort we make to acquire an object, attainment, or praise is consciously or unconsciously done with the goal of being happy. For example, we don't really want to go on vacation. We are really looking for the happiness that we believe the vacation will bring. What if we somehow knew without a doubt that our Hawaiian holiday would be hounded by a hurricane, migraines, a taxi strike, food poisoning, and storm-delayed flights? Would we still look forward to going? It's the same with every endeavor. They are all means to the end of finding happiness.

All our lives, we exert so much effort, travel down so many avenues, to find happiness. We never seem fully satisfied. Our successes are too often and too soon tarnished, or they don't live up to our expectations. Things change. We change. There are many reasons why we don't find what we really want.

Have you ever wondered if life is just a roller coaster ride propelled by craving and the rush of unpredictable, fleeting moments of happiness? What peace and joy we do experience is inevitably followed by the anxiety of holding on to our moment of happiness, disappointment when it fades, or renewed cravings that come packaged with the hope that, *this time* it will be different.

For thousands of years, yogis (as well as the realized individuals of all faith traditions) examined this question, and they discovered an amazing answer...

Peace and Happiness is Within Us as Our True Nature

The deep and fulfilling peace we seek is realized by experiencing our True Self. Obscured by ignorance, it exists within us, waiting to be revealed. This experience is often referred to as Self-realization, enlightenment, or liberation. It is the full integration of every aspect of who we are, and of who we are with the Self. It is the state of being awake.

Ignorance of Our True Nature is the Cause of All Suffering

This is one of the most important truths to understand: suffering is not caused by forces outside of ourselves, but by a faulty and limited perception of life and who we are. Our basic misperception is that we are only a mind encased in a body.

Who we *think* we are is a result of input from innumerable sources: parents, friends, TV, movies, music, books, and Nature. Ignorance also manifests as regarding what's impermanent as permanent and what's painful as pleasant.

Ignorance gives rise to the ego and to endless cravings for things outside ourselves in the hopes of finding happiness. In the end, nothing in Nature is capable of bringing lasting fulfillment. How can we escape this predicament?

Ignorance is Overcome and Happiness Experienced with a Clear, Focused Mind

Just as only a clean undistorted mirror can reflect our face as it truly is, only a one-pointed and tranquil mind can reflect the Self and end ignorance.

All Yoga practices: postures, breathing techniques, deep relaxation, meditation, self-analysis, study, devotion, and selfless service, are designed to help bring the mind to a stillness so clear and steady that it transforms consciousness. All *ideas* about who we are dissolve. The mind, with its countless mazes of thoughts and desires, stills. Our True Self is realized. We experience that we are forever one with the unshakable, eternal ground of existence. It shouldn't be too hard to imagine why this experience is one of supreme peace and joy.

THE TECHNIQUE

You'll notice that this chapter is not very long. The technique of meditation is not complex, but it is a skill that requires practice to perfect.

The heart of the practice is developing the capacity to guide and hold attention. Meditation is *a clear, focused, continuous flow of attention toward an object, image, or thought.* Contrast this with our usual state of mind.

Most of the time, our attention is voluntarily or involuntarily attracted by sense input, thoughts, images, and memories. Our awareness, like a bumblebee searching for nectar, flits from thought to thought: pleasant or unpleasant, beneficial or harmful, useful or useless. Our attention rarely rests in one place very long and hardly ever follows a straight line. What we assume to be a logical flow of thoughts is, on closer examination, a mishmash of mental impressions that insert themselves into our awareness diverting our attention and corrupting the thought process. We don't notice this because these constant mental fluctuations are habit, and because, many of these distracting thoughts come in and out so quickly that they fly below our conscious radar.

The mind's activities seem only partially under our voluntary control. How many times have you thought, "Why does my mind obsess over this?" or "Why can't I keep focused on my work?" The good news is that the mind can be trained. Like training a puppy, it's a matter of persistence and compassion.

Meditation technique consists of three basic elements: choosing an object for meditation, cultivating attentiveness to the object, and overcoming distracting thoughts.

Choosing an object for meditation. The role that the chosen object plays in meditation might best be described by the story of the Fox and the Fleas.

There was a young fox who was infested with fleas. Try as he might, he couldn't get rid of them. He was plagued by intense itchiness that had no relief. He felt that he would lose his mind. One day, a wise old fox came his way. He found our young friend writhing on the ground.

Young friend, what troubles you so?

Fleas! I'm infested with them. I can't sleep. I can't rest. Nothing helps.

Well, son, I think I can help you. But you need to do exactly as I say.

I'm at my wit's end. I'll do whatever you say.

Fine. Take this stick and put it in your mouth. Now walk over to the edge of the pond. Slowly walk into the water, but only until the water reaches your ankles.

The young fox did just as the old fox suggested, although he couldn't imagine what all this had to do with his plight.

OK, son. Now slowly walk in a little deeper, but just up to your knees.

The old fox continued with his instructions, gradually guiding the young one deeper into the pond. Finally, when only his snout, eyes, and stick were above water, he could see that the fleas, to avoid the water, had all gathered on his snout. Now, the old fox's instructions were beginning to make sense.

Go a little deeper until only your nostrils are above the surface. Good. Now take a deep breath and duck underwater so only the stick is above the surface.

The young fox saw that all the fleas were now on the stick. The last instruction was obvious and welcome.

OK, let go of the stick.

The stick is the object of meditation and the fleas are the thoughts that hop in and out of our awareness. The energy of all our thoughts becomes absorbed in the object of meditation. Eventually, in deep meditation, the object of meditation, like the stick, will naturally float away leaving the mind clear and calm.

Since there are hundreds of suitable objects to choose from (see the next chapter), it might seem to be a daunting task, but the underlying principle is simple. *Choose anything that you feel drawn to; an object, image, or thought that you like and that you find inspiring.* The object you choose should remind you of something beyond your daily concerns.

A little care should be taken here. If your hobby is raising orchids, an orchid, although beautiful and uplifting to you, may lead to thoughts of the best fertilizer for your new orchid. You may dearly love your aunt Judy, but meditating on her image may also bring up memories of Thanksgiving dinners, picnics, or even family quarrels. Rather than help focus the attention, these objects may evoke thoughts and memories that distract the mind.

Cultivating clear, steady attention. As mentioned above, the mind is like a bumblebee flitting from flower to flower. Our attention rarely rests anywhere very long. When we meditate, the object of meditation becomes an "anchor thought" for our awareness to rest on, and to return to when it wanders. With some practice, the anchor thought functions as an axis around which all other thoughts revolve. The mind may take flights of fancy, but it knows where its center is and will eventually return there.

An unbroken flow of attention isn't achieved right away. The mind's habit of wandering is deeply rooted.

Overcoming distracting thoughts. Anyone who has tried meditating realizes that a surprising amount of time is spent dwelling on intruding thoughts: everything from a talkative coworker, what's for lunch, the movie you plan to see tonight, your ailing bank account, and your itchy nose. You could describe meditation as the practice of dealing with the distracting thoughts.

There are two ways to deal with these distractions:
- Ignore them
- Analyze them

The technique you will use most is ignoring them. You may be tempted to wrestle your attention back to the object of meditation, but efforts to dominate the mind by force only create tension. This mistaken approach provides the distracting thought with energy by giving it attention. Instead, when you notice that your mind has wandered, *just let go of the distracting thought and refocus the mind on the object of meditation.* It's something like sitting in a movie theater and having someone with a tall hairstyle sit in front of you. The theater is full and you can't move, so you peek over the person's shoulder and focus on the movie. After a while, as you become absorbed in the plot, you forget the hair and are only aware of the movie. Likewise, the intruding thought will slip away when it sees how intent you are on the object of meditation.

Typically, your attention will rest on the object of meditation for a while, and then wander. At some point, you'll notice that it has wandered, and you refocus. This cycle is usually repeated a number of times in each session. It's the same for anyone who meditates.

Meditating has not agitated your mind and your meditation session is not a failure. Not at all. Even with repeated wandering of attention, you can still experience a special peace. This may not happen every sitting, but often enough to encourage you to persevere in the practice.

Stubborn Distracting Thoughts

Sometimes, one thought insists on getting your attention. It doesn't give up. It's like someone repeatedly calling your name outside your office door, demanding attention. When attempts at ignoring this person go nowhere, you put your work aside, let them in, and inquire into what they want. It's the same in meditation. Put the meditation on pause when one very stubborn thought won't leave you alone. Address the thought directly. Without getting up, ask what it wants with you. Why is it coming now and why is it being tenacious? Reason this through. If your mind is presenting a problem that truly needs attention, tell it that you will address it after you meditate.

If the mind still hesitates to return its focus on the object of meditation, you can remind it of the benefits of meditating. For inspiration, recall past satisfying sessions and the examples of great yogis and sages who have travelled this path. Your mind will be both educated and placated. You will have gained its trust and it will become more cooperative in the future.

It Bears Repeating

One of the most common pitfalls that new meditators face is the inclination to be aggressive with the mind. Don't confuse enthusiasm, strength, clear determination, and steadfast persistence with a rough tough, don't-give-the-mind-an-inch-or-it-will-be-sorry approach.

Be kind, nonjudgmental, and loving to yourself. Meditation should be peaceful and noncompetitive. Don't put undue pressure on yourself to reach a lofty goal all at once. The longest journey begins with the first step.

Even a little success in meditation brings results that far outweigh the effort. The simple act of sitting for your allotted time, even if your mind remains restless and scattered, is still a formidable agent for positive change in your life. Don't give up. Attend to and enjoy the process.

Never force the mind in meditation.

OBJECTS FOR MEDITATION

Yoga tradition offers a wide variety of objects for meditation. Indulge your sense of adventure and experiment with whatever you are drawn to. Don't rush the search. The object you choose will become a daily companion on your inner journey. You will look forward to spending time with it. It becomes a source of strength, stability, and comfort.

No object is better than any other. Sometimes, teachers might say that a particular technique is best. They do this to inspire faith in their students, and this is a good thing if properly understood. You *should* feel that the form of meditation you practice is the best *for you*. Keep in mind, that the object or technique doesn't meditate. The mind does. The best object is the one that works for you.

You can choose anything you like as long as:
- It is something you like
- It is uplifting to you

The process of choosing an object can be compared to dating and marriage. Dating is, in part, a learning process. You become familiar with the habits and personalities of others and learn what you're looking for in a partner. At some point during the dating stage you feel the urge to settle down with someone you've gotten to know and love. It's much the same with an object of meditation. Date a few techniques. One day, you'll feel attracted to one and have the urge to settle down with it. In the long run, it's best to find one object and stick to it.[2] Sticking to one object brings success faster. We accumulate conscious and subconscious associations by using the same object daily. This accumulated storehouse of mental impressions creates a natural inclination to go deeper in meditation more quickly. Meditation becomes increasingly easier and productive.

Try practicing with an object for at least a week or two to get a feel for it before experiencing another. Repeat the process as many times as you like until you feel drawn to one. If after a long while, you can't choose, but feel the need to settle on one practice, it is best to seek the advice of an adept or master in whom you have faith. The principle

---

[2] There are schools of Yoga and meditation that use a variety of techniques. If you belong to one such school, follow that path. Every path is self-contained with an internal harmony and logic that provides what is needed to progress.

is the same whether you choose the object yourself or have someone choose for you. It is a matter of faith in your ability to select an object for meditation, or for someone to choose for you.

Even after you've chosen an object, you can still benefit from using others from time to time. For example, in a group meditation, for the sake of unity (and to expand your horizons), you could use whatever object the group is using. These are not departures from your daily routine, but valuable side-trips for learning. We can gain useful insights when we step outside of our daily patterns. At the same time we should always know where our home is, where our roots are, where our strength lies.

We can divide the objects used for meditation into four categories: visualization, sound, inquiry, and body centered. These categories, and the objects in each, have been passed down through lineages of Yoga masters and verified by countless practitioners over millennia.

VISUALIZATION

Visualization can be practiced with open-eyed gazing or by holding an image in the mind's eye. Objects typically used for open-eyed gazing include yantras[3] or mandalas, images of deities or enlightened beings, a candle flame, the infinite expanse of the sky, the vastness of the ocean, a cross, Star of David, or any holy symbol. It is also common to visualize light (generally white or golden light) or to "see" a mantra (its letters) at one of the higher chakras as you repeat it. (*Chakras are explained below.*)

Gazing (*tradak*)

This technique begins by holding a steady gaze on an object. Have the object at eye level. Try not to blink. Keep the focus soft. Be careful not to strain the eyes. If you begin to feel any tension, discomfort, or fatigue, close the eyes while holding the vision of the image within (this is the visualization part). When the inner image fades, open the eyes and return to gazing. Continue with this cycle for the duration of the sitting.

If you are using an image of a deity, you can move your gaze to its different parts and symbols. Begin with the feet, and then move to the legs, torso, head and face, and end with the arms and hands. Notice the facial features, garments, colors, and any adornments.[4] Then close your eyes and try to "see" the image. If you can't see it at all or it is dim or fading, repeat the gazing and try visualizing again.

As you gaze and visualize, you can repeat a mantra specific to that deity and reflect on its divine attributes (such as omniscience, mercy, unconditional love). Devotional feelings inspire and focus the mind.

A classic object for tradak is a candle flame. It has an advantage over other objects. The light of the flame remains on the retina when you close your eyes, giving you an actual image to focus on. Gently gaze at the flame without blinking. Close the eyes and try to retain the image of the flame within.

---

[3] A yantra is a geometric design representing the energies of the cosmos (macrocosm) and the individual's place in it (microcosm). The visible form of a mantra, it helps focus the mind. It is similar to a mandala.

[4] Adornments of deities, as well as objects held, setting, and colors have symbolic meaning. Knowing what they represent enhances your meditation experience. If this interests you, you can find books on the symbolism of many faith traditions online.

In addition to being a meditation technique, tradak is a way to purify the subtle nerve currents (*nadis*) around the eyes and strengthen vision.

Visualization

If you have been practicing the open-eyed method for some time and can hold the inner image fairly well, you can skip the open-eye gazing and work only with visualization. Continue with the same object you used for tradak, using the open-eye gazing if the attention wanders too far.

Visualizations can also be done without the support of any external object. For example, you could picture a golden light – the light of love, wisdom, and compassion – at the center of your heart, removing darkness from your life and radiating to all.

Chakras. Chakras (centers of consciousness) are commonly used for visualizations. Although included in this section, they could also be considered part of body centered meditation.

There are seven principle chakras. They are in the subtle body, at points that correspond to locations along the spine. Each chakra (literally, *wheel*) is like a command center for different aspects of consciousness. Chakras, starting at the base of the spine and moving up, represent the evolution of human consciousness from instinctive animal-like attributes, to human qualities, to Cosmic Consciousness.

- *Muladhara*, the root chakra, is located at the base of the spine and concerns itself with matters of self-preservation.
- *Swadisthana*, the sacral chakra, is at the area of the genitals and pertains to procreation and the psychological matters that go with it.
- *Manipura*, the third chakra, is at the navel. It is concerned with social issues and group dynamics. Its focus is our place within our family, coworkers, and community. The consciousness of this chakra seeks to make the best of our place on the social scales of youngest - oldest, brightest - dullest, tallest - shortest, strongest - sickest, wealthiest - poorest, most talented - least talented, shyest - boldest, etc. Though not necessarily negative, the focus of this chakra tends toward self-interest.
- *Anahata*, the heart chakra, is at the center of the midline of the sternum. At this level, higher human qualities begin to manifest.

Compassion for others begins here. It is the center for selfless love, kindness, and empathy.
- *Vishuddha*, the fifth chakra, is at the base of the throat. It is associated with the part of the mind that takes in impressions for analysis.
- *Ajna*, is at the third eye, the space between the eyebrows (or more correctly inside the center of the head at the level of the space between the eyebrows). This is the seat of the mind, the center of self-awareness, the root of individual consciousness.
- *Sahasrara*, the highest chakra, is at the crown of the head. It is the center for Cosmic Consciousness. At this level, ignorance and limitation are left behind and unity with the Self is experienced.

Each chakra has a mantra, yantra, deity, and color associated with it. You *could* do the research to find out which mantra or color to use for the first chakra. Awaken that chakra, go to the second, and continue in this way until you reach the top. This practice is complex, subtle, and can lead to complications. It's not recommended unless given to you by a master whose teachings include this approach. Here's why...

Focused attention on a chakra intensifies its content. The energy released in deep meditation is neutral, but very powerful.[5] It amplifies the state of consciousness at a chakra, whether it is positive or negative.

A chakra becomes fully activated when it is purified of selfish impressions. Awakening a lower chakra prematurely – if it is not purified of selfishness – can cause problems. That's why our attention should be centered on a higher chakra, from the heart up. Higher chakras control the lower ones. Keep your aim high and you'll get the full benefit. Lower chakras *are* used in meditation, but should only be done if you are part of a tradition that includes this practice.

It should be noted that you don't need to meditate on a chakra to open it. Any technique or object of meditation, coupled with a life of lovingkindness, will awaken the chakras naturally and safely.

---

[5] The powerful energy of evolution within each individual is the *kundalini*. See the *Sanskrit Glossary*.

SOUND

This category includes listening to sounds outside or inside the body, and mantra repetition. Regardless of which technique you choose, it's a sound practice.

Listening to Sound Outside the Body

This consists of sounds that are conducive to a relaxed, alert state, such as gentle waves breaking on the shore or leaves rustling in a breeze.

To practice this technique, bring your attention to the chosen sound. Let the sound float into your awareness. Don't name or analyze it. Refrain from poetic musings or mental descriptions of what you are listening to. Just notice the sound as it comes to you without effort.

Listening to Sound Within

Sounds heard within are called *nada*. They are variations of the omnipresent humming of OM, the primordial vibration of the creation, evolution, and dissolution of the universe. It is heard when the mind is deeply focused and clear, and the subtle nerve currents, the *nadis*, are purified.

The nada manifests in different ways according to the depth of the meditation and the temperament of the meditator. As the practitioner listens to the nada, its character may change. For example, the first manifestation may sound like a conch blowing. Focusing on that sound may lead to the sound of rumbling thunder. As you continue with this practice, more sounds will be revealed over time, culminating with the pure, deep hum of OM (*more details on* OM *below*).

You can sit in a quiet space and carefully listen for the nada or it may also manifest naturally in other forms of meditation.

Mantras

Mantras (literally, *to protect the mind*) are sound syllables representing aspects of the Divine. They are not words used to label objects. As such, they are not part of language. Focused repetition of a mantra is the basis of Japa Yoga, the Yoga of Repetition.

Mantra repetition is certainly one of the most common forms of meditation. The reason is because mantras are both easy to use and remarkably effective. Mantras uplift the mind and bring powerful healing energy to the body. They open the heart and create harmony where there is strife. The vibrations of mantras can be transferred to an object or environment. They grant virtues and all spiritual benefits. How can sound do all this?

Sounds can soothe or agitate. Many people shudder when they hear a metal utensil scrape the bottom of a metal pan. At the same time, countless vacationers seek out the shoreline to let the sound of the waves soothe their tattered nerves. Mantras are sounds that calm and strengthen the mind. They were not invented by anyone. Sages in deep meditative states experienced aspects of the cosmic vibration. The sounds they heard, that were integral to these states, are mantras. The mantras we repeat are facsimiles of the original vibration that they perceived. Mantra repetition gradually tunes the mind to that vibration and the corresponding meditative state.

The vibration within. Every branch of Yoga purifies and strengthens a different aspect of our nature and applies it to the attainment of Self-realization. Karma Yoga addresses our active and social side; Bhakti Yoga, devotion; Jnana Yoga, the part of us that is drawn to inquiry and understanding; Hatha Yoga, the physical side; and Raja Yoga, the will. How does Japa Yoga fit into this principle?

There are universal wordless vocalizations that are inborn responses to events in life. These sounds are a deep-rooted way for us to communicate (a scream is a call for help), restore inner harmony when we are in discomfort (moaning helps tolerate pain), or express and amplify joy in good times (laughter). We sigh in relief, gasp in surprise, cry in grief, make a yummy sound when eating something tasty, and, in one of the most beautiful expressions of the human spirit, we hum or whistle when we're content. Pre-word communications are an integral part of who we are.

If laughter is the sound of joy, and moans the sound of pain, what is the sound of the Absolute as it manifests in the depths of the mind? Mantras. The mantras we repeat are vocalizations of various aspects of Ishwara and the cosmic cycle of creation.[6]

Some mantras represent the all-pervading omniscient, omnipresent, and omnipotent aspects of the creative process. Other mantras express

---

[6]The Absolute is called Brahman. It is infinite, nameless, formless, and beyond dualities. All creation begins when Brahman expresses as sound (then Brahman is then called Ishwara, creator or lord). The phases of creation (generation, evolution, and dissolution) are contained in the cosmic hum: pranava or OM (*Yoga Sutras*, 1.27). All sounds come from, return to, and rest in OM.

specific sub-phases of the creation cycle that resonate on a deeply human level. We experience them as virtues, blessings, or other Divine qualities, such as:
- Abundance (the infinite variety and possibilities of creation)
- Auspiciousness (signals that good things are about to come)
- Supreme peace (the stillness behind the creative process)
- Unconditional love (drawing together in harmony, different, often paradoxical facets of creation)
- Joy (the inherent rightness of creation[7])
- Compassion (resonance)
- Wisdom (cosmic order)
- Freedom (forces that remove obstacles)

Mantras are the vibrations of these qualities (or energies). When we repeat a mantra, we generate a pulsation in the mind that resonates with the vibration of that quality. Take, for example, shanti. Like every mantra, it is not separate from OM, but a facet of it that is already vibrating within us. Shanti is not the absence of conflict or tension, but a peace beyond understanding. We normally don't experience shanti because the mind is too active and distracted. Our mind's activities act like static that obscure subtler truths. By focused repetition of shanti, the mind resonates with that vibration and becomes calmer and clearer. Eventually we connect with the inner vibration of shanti and experience it in its fullness.

Bija mantras (see *Personal Mantras*, below) are also aspects of the cosmic vibration. They exist on a level that cannot be translated into words. They come close to expressing the inexpressible Absolute.

Mantras' special power is the ability to reach the mind on its deepest level. They help us transcend (but not contradict) the rational mind and dive to the core of our being.

Two classes of mantras. There are several ways to classify mantras, but perhaps the most important is by intention. *Kamya* mantras are repeated with the intent of attaining worldly gain: wealth, health, a child, a new home, etc. The goal is limited in scope and benefit. The problem with this approach, can be summed up by the well-known saying: "Be careful what you wish for – you might get it." Even a superficial review of our lives will reveal that we often don't know what's best for us. The higher category is *nishkamya*, mantras

---

[7] See *ananda* in the *Sanskrit Glossary*.

repeated without limited objectives. They are repeated only to remove ignorance and attain Self-realization. The mantras recommended in this book are from the nishkamya category.

Choosing a mantra. Once you choose a mantra, you make the best progress if you stick to it for life. You can select a mantra because you are drawn to its sound vibration, its meaning, or because it is associated with a particular deity with whom you feel a strong connection. For example, OM *Namah Sivaya* is a mantra connected with the deity, Siva. Devotees of Lord Siva often use that mantra. Their devotional feelings energize their practice and help keep the mind inspired and focused. However, since the word *siva* means auspiciousness, the repetition of this mantra is not restricted to devotees. If you don't feel a connection to Siva, the deity, but are drawn to that vibration or meaning, you could certainly use that mantra. For you, it is not a devotional practice. Mantras transcend associations with deities. They are sound formulas whose fundamental benefit derives from their vibration, not associated ideas or images.

Personal mantras. If you have heard of someone receiving a mantra that's been selected just for her or him, it's what is usually referred to as a personal mantra. Often, but not always, they are given to those who enter into the guru/disciple relationship at the time of their *diksha* (initiation).[8] There isn't a unique mantra for every person. In some traditions, several mantras are used for diksha, in others, the same mantra is given to all of their students.

Diksha mantras are often from a special category, known as *bija* (seed) mantras. They are pure sound vibration and have no translatable meaning. A bija mantra is "activated" during the initiation and the vibration of the mantra is transmitted to the student to jump-start their practice.

Because of their power, bija mantras are normally not given unless the student is living a lifestyle that supports the changes that these powerful mantras can set into motion. The guru/disciple relationship brings with it expert guidance and the support of a community of like-minded seekers.

The technique. Since mantras work with sound vibration, proper pronunciation ensures the greatest benefits. The repetition should be

---

[8] For more regarding initiation and the guru/disciple relationship, please refer to the chapter, *Is a Guru Necessary?*

clear and consistent. Listen to every syllable as you repeat it. Keep the tune the same throughout the session (see below, *Mantras to try*, for more on the tune). Repeat it at a pace that's not too slow or quick. To help your focus, you can visualize the mantra as you repeat it. Continue, repeating the mantra from the beginning to the end of your session.

"M" and "n" sounds are important. Many mantras contain these sounds because they raise the vibration to the crown chakra. Try repeating a mantra that contains either or both of these letters while holding the palm of one hand on the crown of the head. If you are doing it correctly, you'll feel a vibration there.

Mantras that include the "a" sound ("ah" or like the "u" in but) are also common. It is a sound that opens the heart. Keep the throat relaxed when repeating this sound. Opening the heart doesn't means that you will have an emotional experience. It is about stepping away from the ego to develop a heightened receptivity to the promptings of the higher wisdom.

"R" sounds should be slightly rolled, like a very soft "d" sound. For example, Hari is pronounced as, hah – dee.

The main idea is to keep your entire sound-making apparatus relaxed. That way the sounds will be open and full.[9] Even when mantra repetition is done silently, the same guidelines apply.

The mantra can be repeated out loud, silently with lip movement, or just mentally. Out loud is easiest, but not as powerful as with lip movement. Repeating the mantra within is the most powerful, but is a little more difficult than the other two methods since there is less physical and aural reinforcement of the sound vibration. You can begin out loud for several weeks or months, progress to lip movement, and then silently within. You can also use all three techniques in a single session to help gradually bring the mind to focused attention, returning to lip movement or verbal repetition if the mind becomes restless. There's no rush. Enjoy the process.

It's easy to regard mantra meditation as a daunting repetitive act. Repeating one mantra over and over, with no variation, might seem monotonous. In truth, as your focus deepens, you'll find nothing monotonous about the growing clarity and peace.

---

[9] Everybody has a "key note," the most natural sound they are built to reproduce. When we make that sound, the entire body vibrates, bringing physical and psychological benefits. Just open the mouth, and with the face, throat, and abdomen completely relaxed, exhale and make a sound. When you get it right, you'll feel the vibration.

You also don't have to approach mantra japa as a long string of repetitions. Instead, say the mantra once. Just once. Resolve to hear every syllable, every letter. Say it once with full awareness. Stay relaxed; don't force the mind. Say it again and now again, each time approaching it as if you only need repeat it one time. Continue until the end of your sitting. If you repeat the mantra just once with full awareness and faith, Self-realization will be yours.

Mantra repetition is not a mindless parroting of a sound, but an attentive act set against a background of enthusiasm. For keen seekers, each and every repetition is a moment of connection with the Self, an affirmation of the Truth of their own spiritual identity and a reminder of their intentions.

Mala beads. A practical aid to mantra practice is the use of *mala* beads. Malas are used like rosary beads. With each repetition of the mantra, advance one bead. The mala is held in the right hand and draped over the middle or ring finger. Since the index finger represents the selfish ego, it's best to keep it out of the practice. Slide one bead at a time toward yourself without using the index finger.

Most malas are made from one hundred-eight, fifty-four, or twenty-seven beads plus one more (the *meru*) that usually has a tassel attached. The meru represents the highest truth. Since you cannot go higher than the highest, when you reach that bead, instead of going over it, flip the string of beads and begin again. If you note how long it takes to do a string of malas you can use it as a timing device for your meditation. Many practitioners also wear their beads during the day to remind them of their spiritual aspirations and because the beads, having absorbed the vibrations of the mantra, help keep the mind calm and clear.

Likhit Japa. Another way of working with a mantra is *Likhit Japa*, mantra writing. In this practice, you mindfully write the mantra as you repeat it. It is an effective method to increase the power of concentration. Writing the mantra reinforces the mental repetition: you think it, say it, write it, see it. Be neat and unless it is a long mantra, don't break up the mantra between two lines.

You can write a certain number of pages per sitting or write for an allotted number of minutes.

If you are artistic, you can write the mantra in colors and make beautiful designs.

Mantras to try. Mantras are not limited to Sanskrit or Yoga. Repetition of powerful sounds and prayers are found in most spiritual traditions. If you know a melody for a mantra, you can use it. If not, it's fine to repeat it in a monotone with the syllables slightly prolonged.

- **OM**. OM is the source of all mantras. It is the primordial vibration from which all sounds originate. Most, but not all mantras used for meditation contain OM. In Sanskrit, it is three letters: "A," "U," and "M." OM rhymes with "home" since the "A" and "U," when combined, become a long "O" sound.

  To pronounce the "A," you simply open the mouth and make a deep, natural sound, almost like a sigh. All audible sound begins with this action. It represents creation. The "U" is formed when the sound rolls forward toward the lips with the help of the tongue and cheeks. This represents evolution. Finally, to make the "M" sound, the lips come together. This last sound represents dissolution. So together "A," "U," and "M" signify creation, evolution, and dissolution – the entire cycle of life.

  According to the philosophy of Advaita Vedanta (the philosophical school of nondualism), "A" = outer consciousness, "U" = inner consciousness and "M" = superconsciousness. The same three letters also signify the waking, dreaming, and dreamless deep sleep states. Beyond these three states is a fourth (*turiya*[10]), the transcendent witness consciousness.

  Yoga recognizes OM as the sound manifestation of Ishwara.[11] Ishwara can be understood as the limitless God (Brahman) perceived from within the limitations of creation.

  OM should be repeated in an easy relaxed way. It's not singing. Keep the body relaxed, and after taking a deep inhalation, begin the chant. Half the time should be on "O" and half on "M."

  Sri Swami Satchidananda on OM:

  "We should understand that OM was not invented by anybody. Some people didn't come together, hold nominations, take a vote, and the majority decided, "All right, let God have the name OM." No. He or She manifested as OM. Any seeker who really wants to see God face to face will ultimately see Him as OM. That is why it transcends all geographical, political or

---

[10] For more on *turiya*, see the chapter on *The Four States of Consciousness*.

[11] For more on *Ishwara*, refer to *Yoga Sutras*, 1. 23 - 1.28, and the *Sanskrit Glossary*.

theological limitations. It doesn't belong to one country or one religion; it belongs to the entire universe.

It is a variation of this OM that we see as the "Amen" or "Ameen," which the Christians, Muslims and Jews say. That doesn't mean someone changed it. Truth is always the same. Wherever you sit for meditation, you will ultimately end in experiencing OM or the hum. But when you want to express what you experienced, you may use different words according to your capacity or the language you know."

- **OM Shanti** (shahn tee), OM Peace.
- **Hari OM.** Although Hari used as a name for the deity Vishnu, the preserver, it is often repeated simply for the value of its vibration. Hari releases energy from the solar plexus and helps bring it upward to the throat. OM takes that vibration, strengthens it, and brings it to the crown of the head and above. Hari OM helps remove inner obstacles.
- **Soham**, "I am That." Soham repeats naturally with each inhalation (*so*), and exhalation (*hum*). Because this repetition is automatic, constant, and natural, it is referred to as *ajapa japa*, the repetition without repeating. You begin by repeating the mantra, and as the mind becomes clear and focused, you can hear it repeating within.
- **Shalom**, Hebrew for peace. It is noteworthy that the vibration of Shalom and OM Shanti are similar in sound and meaning.
- **Maranatha**, "Lord, come." This Aramaic word is the mantra suggested by Father John Main, a Benedictine Monk who learned meditation in India and later founded the World Community for Christian Meditation.
- **Ave Maria**, Hail Mary. These two words alone can be used as a mantra, or you can repeat the entire prayer.
- **OM Namah**[12] **Sivaya** (OM namah shee-vuh-yah). "OM, Salutations to Siva." Siva is the third in the Hindu trinity of Brahma (creator), Vishnu (preserver), and Siva (transformer or dissolver). It is commonly repeated by devotees of Siva. Meaning auspiciousness, it can be repeated without devotional thoughts of Lord Siva.

---

[12] Namah means salutations and is included in many mantras. The word is the root of the common greeting, *namaste*, which means "salutations to you." There is another, beautiful meaning for namaste: *na + ma + te*, not me, you. It is a reminder to shift our focus from ourselves in order to serve another.

- **OM Mani Padme Hum** (OM, manee, padmay, hum – the "u" is like the double "o" in book). This mantra is widely used by Tibetan Buddhists. Not much importance is placed on the meaning of the words. OM and Hum cannot be translated, they are repeated for their vibratory effect. Mani and padme, taken together, mean "Jewel in the lotus." The lotus is symbolic of spiritual wisdom. Therefore, the jewel in the lotus suggests the highest spiritual attainment.
- **Bismillah Al-Rahman, Al-Rahim**, a mantra from Islam. It translates as, "In the name of Allah, most compassionate, most merciful."

Advantages of Mantra Meditation
- The sound of the mantra calms and focuses the mind.
- It is portable; you don't need to carry anything with you.
- Bring your mantra with you during the day. Mantra repetition can be done during other activities (cooking, mowing the lawn) or throughout stressful events (going to the dentist).
- Use mantra to send healing, comforting vibrations to those in need.

Repeating your mantra during an activity is beneficial. It helps recall and reestablish the meditative mood of your formal sitting. However, it is not normally considered as a replacement for formal, seated meditation.

PRAYER

Often misused or misunderstood, prayer stands on its own as a meditation practice or it can be an important adjunct to meditation.

Prayer begins as a word centered activity, usually asking God for something we want or need. We make requests for help in finding a mate, a cure, to pass our exam, or for success in our work. We also pray for forgiveness, to give thanks, and to express love and adoration for God. Prayer sometimes consists of wordless communication as we experience laughter, tears of regret, gratitude, or joy. Whatever form our prayer may take, it is about communing with God. It is the individual yearning to connect with his or her source and home.

There is a dimension of prayer that is deeper still, when all words and emotions subside; when intense yearning and communing lead to silence. We are in the heart of prayer when asking, praising, speaking, and thinking have reached their limits. There are no longer any expectations of an answer from above, of comfort, or of peace. We watch and listen, being alert and fully present to a vast, stark silence. We can do little else but surrender. In that surrender, we drop the burden of thinking we are, or need to be, in control of every aspect of life.[13] Emptied of all expectations, the heart finds the courage to open, and we find ourselves drawn into the silence, not by force, but by love. Through love we find the willingness to give ourselves to the experience freely and completely. We stand before the Infinite, struck still, ready for the Divine embrace that dissolves all separateness.

The true story of the Old Man of Ars is about such prayer. This elderly gentleman was observed by Saint John Vianney, the pastor of a church in France. Day after day, the old man would sit in the pew for hours, utterly peaceful and still, radiating a special peace. One day St. John asked the man what he was doing while he sat there. The old man replied, "I just sit and look at God and He looks at me."

Prayer practiced in this way, shares much with the practice of Self-inquiry (see below). Prayer uses a devotional mood to bring us to an alert silence that is beyond the workings of the mind. Self-inquiry uses the discriminative intellect to do the same.

---

[13] This life strategy seldom works well. For it to be a successful, we would need to know the ultimate outcome of every decision and act, know all the pertinent information at every turn in life, and have unerring judgement.

A more practical way of living would be to do our best, guided by proven moral, ethical, and spiritual guidelines, and then leave the rest to God.

SELF-INQUIRY

Self-inquiry is a fascinating form of meditation. At its heart, it's about tracking down the source of the feeling of "I, me, and mine." "*My* house, *my* life, *my* partner, *my* passion, *my* experience, *my* accomplishments, *my* body, *my* mind" – you refer to all these experiences, every experience – as possessions. The owner of something is not the same as the object owned. Anything you can touch, taste, see, hear, smell, imagine, or remember cannot be who you are. Anything that is observed is the *object* of perception. The real you, the Self, is the *subject*.[14]

Who is the owner, the witness of our lives? What part of us watches as we experience happiness and suffering, grow old, and then pass away? In other words, "Who am I?"

Self-inquiry makes use of the mind's discriminative capacity (*buddhi*) as a tool for meditation. It is a technique that involves a deep examination of the mind, the nature of awareness, and the Self. Gradually, the limitations of the mind are recognized and transcended, culminating in Self-realization.

A well known approach for practicing self-inquiry is reflection on the question, "Who am I?" Begin this process by asking this question of yourself. Then examine the responses your mind presents, eliminating answers that don't represent the true "I," the witness of all phenomena. Here's an abridged sample of the kind of questions you would ask yourself:

Who am I? Am I my legs?
No, I seem to be the owner of my legs.
Am I my arms?
No, I don't seem to be limited to a part of the body.
Am I my body?
Again, I seem to be the owner of the body. I even say, "My body."
 Therefore, I am not the body, but the owner of the body.
Am I my intellect?
When I study and learn, I am aware of the process. Whatever 'I" am,
 it seems to be witnessing the intellect while it learns.

---

[14] In the *Yoga Sutras*, subject and object are also referred to as, Seer and seen, Owner and owned, and Purusha and Prakriti. We could also substitute Spirit and Nature, or consciousness and matter for the same principles.

Am I the mind itself?
Well, at this moment I'm watching my mind as it goes through this analysis. Again, I seem to be the owner or witness of the mind. I even say, "My mind." I can't be the mind.

The idea is not to reflexively say, "No," or give a stock yogic answer, but to observe the content of your consciousness after the question is asked. Be open, objective, and patient. Simply look for the "I," the sense of self. Where is it? Somewhere in the body? The body itself? Is it the mind or part of the mind? Who's asking these questions? Who's answering them? Continue asking questions and observing. After exhausting your questions, just observe the mind. You will find it more peaceful, focused, and open, even though you didn't hit on the ultimate answer. Depending on how long your meditation session is, you can repeat the entire routine.

Don't let the questioning become a source of frustration. It's not a philosophical obstacle course. Think of this technique as an exercise in exploration and investigation, a process of awakening, amplifying, and refining awareness. The questions help you become familiar with your notions of what constitutes you. They are a necessary first stage, but you won't be relying on them always.

The next stage is deeper and more fulfilling, pure wordless observation. Simply sit with a calm, focused mind, and look within. Through pure observation, seek the source of the "I" feeling. Be alert to the present moment, open and ready to receive without judgment. When the attention is clear and steady, the discriminative aspect of the mind will naturally search for the source of individual consciousness.

Over time, you will find yourself approaching the outer borders of the intellect and the mind's inability to grasp the ultimate (infinite) truth. At the same time you will experience a growing a sense of something transcendent, a deeper reality that is more solid, stable, wiser, and powerful – more "you" – than anything you've ever experienced. Words can never convey this, but we can say that it is radical in its impact. While the experience is transcendent, it carries a clear sense of, "Of course. This is who I really am. I'm not the one who has been searching, but the one watching the search. Why didn't I see it before? It's so obvious."

Enlightenment is extraordinary – *extra - ordinary*. The great paradox of this exercise is that what we are looking for is what is doing the looking. What we seek is who we already are.

BODY CENTERED MEDITATION

This category includes objects of meditation such as the chakras,[15] the breath (discussed below), and the postures of Hatha Yoga.

Hatha Yoga

Our minds spend much of the day focused on bodily sensations and activities. Because of this habit, a high percentage of what distracts attention in meditation is body centered. Aches, stiffness, and restlessness are familiar distractions to many meditators. The stretching and bending of Hatha Yoga postures address these physical obstacles. Proper performance of asanas is as much about cultivating mental poise and focus as it is about making the body more supple, strong, and healthy. The regular practice of Hatha Yoga brings the body and mind to a harmonious state: dynamic, relaxed, balanced, and stable. The mind is better prepared to meditate and the body ceases to be a hindrance.

The Breath

There's an intimate relationship between the mind and the breath. The pace, rhythm, and depth of our breathing is a reflection of our state of mind. When we are anxious, the breathing becomes more rapid or irregular. When we are in a calm, clear state, the breath becomes more subtle and regular. By observing the breath, we tune into subtle aspects of the mind.

Meditation techniques using breath observation:
- Watch the inhalation and exhalation of each breath from its very beginning to end. Simply follow the flow of the breath in and out of the body.
- Feel that the breath is flowing into the body from the top of the head down to the base of the spine as you inhale, and from the base of the spine out through the top of the head as you exhale. If you are not drawn to the breath flowing in and out of the top of our head, substitute your nose.
- Have the awareness at the abdomen. Feel its movement as you breathe in and out. If you like, you could add the words, "rise" or "in" as you inhale, and "fall" or "out" as you exhale.

---
[15] See the chapter, *Visualizations*

- Count the breaths. When you reach ten, start over from one.
- Combine breath awareness with an affirmation. With every exhalation, feel that you are exhaling a trait or habit you wish to eliminate. As you inhale, feel that you are inhaling the opposite trait. For example, you can exhale fear and inhale faith.
- Combine watching the breath with mantra repetition. Be sure to add the mantra to the rhythm of the breath and not change the pattern of breathing to fit your repetition of the mantra.

In any form of meditation, when the body and mind become very still, the rate of breathing becomes slower. You need less prana (vital energy) to operate. Your need for oxygen also drops, so the breathing becomes very subtle. With an even stiller mind, the breathing will pause for a few seconds, or even longer. When the mind's activities wind down even more, the breathing stops. When the mind returns to a more active state or when the body needs to breathe, the breath will resume its usual movements. The breath stopping is a sign that your meditations are maturing; the mind is becoming absorbed in the object of meditation.

Walking Meditation

This technique is best experienced in Nature. It can be done in a group or alone. It can combine physical movement with mantra, and breath.

Before beginning the walk, do some pranayama, chants, and affirmations. Then you're ready to go.

The basic idea is to walk mindfully, feeling the weight shift from heel to toe, and from one foot to the next. If you are walking with a group, have everyone line up, one behind the other, about six feet apart. Hold the gaze on the heels of the person in front of you and coordinate your pace with him or her.

Keep a moderate, steady pace. Arms can be relaxed at the sides moving naturally, or the hands can be folded in front of the chest.

Repeat a mantra with each step if you like. Divide the syllables in any way that is natural to you. You can do the same with the breathing, combining the inhalations and exhalations in any way you prefer. Mantra and breathing can both be added to the walking.

After a certain time or distance, sit for a few moments to feel the peace. Add closing chants.

HOW TO COMBINE TECHNIQUES

Most meditation techniques can be combined to good effect. Mantra with visualizations, breath with mantras, and visualizations with breath are just a few examples. There are advantages to combining techniques. By using more than one faculty of awareness at a time (sight, sound, body sensations), you will be giving the mind a wider allowable circle in which to focus. The mind can move between two or three points that are related to your meditation.

Little by little, the mind will attain one-pointedness. You'll find over time, the mind will gradually incline toward one object. For example, if you have been combining mantra with the breath, there will come a time, when awareness of the mantra or the breath may naturally fade away.

Take your time and enjoy your exploration and experimentation.

BUILDING BLOCKS FOR SUCCESS IN MEDITATION

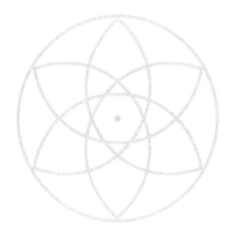

WHERE TO MEDITATE

It's helpful if you can set aside a separate room for meditation. Decorate it so that it inspires you and reminds you of your intent. Every time you enter, thoughts and feelings regarding meditation will naturally arise. The space itself stores the vibrations of previous meditations and jump-starts your practice every time you sit.

Creating a sacred space is important. Every time you turn to it, you affirm the importance of your spiritual pursuits by putting all other aspects of you life on pause. Your spiritual well-being deserves prominent attention and nurturing.

If you don't have a separate room, any quiet space where you can reasonably expect to be undisturbed will be fine. An unused closet or even a corner of a room will work well. Don't get stuck searching for an absolutely perfect spot. You can even use a box to hold your meditation paraphernalia and just open it when it is time to meditate. Be practical.

Here are a few helpful hints.

- If you have a corner to spare, you can create a sacred space by having a small cabinet to house your pictures, candles, and incense. Open the door only when you meditate, and close it when you're done. If even this is not possible, you are not lost. Find the best place in your home and forge ahead with your practice. Without a doubt, your persistence will overcome the shortcomings of the space.

  If you live in a noisy area, don't despair. It can be a blessing in disguise. Although it might take you a little longer to experience some of the benefits of meditation, you will develop great strength of mind. You'll gain the ability to meditate in any setting. I first practiced meditation when I lived directly across the street from a busy railroad station. I'll never regret the experience. Soon I was no longer prone to be distracted by outside sounds.

- Incense helps to purify the atmosphere, uplifts the spirit, and calms the mind.
- Environment is stronger than will. Create a peaceful haven by including objects that inspire you. You can use images of a deity you feel devotion towards, your guru, inspiring photos of nature, candles, and fresh or artificial flowers. (Dried flowers are

BUILDING BLOCKS FOR SUCCESS IN MEDITATION

not recommended. They have little prana – after all, they are corpses.)
- The room should not be too warm or too cool. Too warm, and you will tend to get sleepy. Too cool, and the discomfort will distract the mind.
- Paint the room a soft, tranquil color, a light blue, green, cream, or gold, for example. It's generally best to avoid bright or intense colors that can stir the mind into activity.
- Have an illumined clock to keep track of the time and an egg timer to signal the end of the session. You don't want the mind to be preoccupied with being late for work or an appointment.
- If your space allows it, face east or north. This aligns you with energy currents that help calm and focus the mind. When you face east, you are aligning your energy with the earth's rotational flow. There is also a magnetic force that manifests from the north to the south pole. Facing north puts you in an alignment with these energies and benefits meditation.

   Meditating facing east or north also gives a boost to your meditation as you join countless meditators worldwide who are facing in the same direction.
- Take advantage of places outside the home that are conducive to meditation. Quiet spots in the woods, caves, near a waterfall, river, shoreline, at or near a mountaintop, a holy site or temple, or anywhere where seekers have traditionally gone to practice. If you are in one of these spots, sit at least for a little while. It can boost your practice.

HOW YOU SIT MAKES A DIFFERENCE

Before Sitting

It helps to take a bath or shower or at least splash water on the face, neck, hands, and forearms. Cool water awakens the mind and absorbs negative energy, washing it away.

Clean, loose-fitting clothes help ensure comfort. It's helpful, but not necessary, to have clothing worn only for meditation.

It's important to maintain a comfortable, stable posture for the duration of your sitting. The seat should be high enough to take pressure off your knees and hips. You can sit on a folded blanket or a pillow that is not too soft. Many yogis place a wool cloth over their seat. Wool helps insulate the body from cold and the downward pull of the earth's energy. If sitting on the floor is uncomfortable for you, sit in a straight back chair. It is easier to sit with your back erect on that kind of chair rather than an easy chair.

Lying down is not recommended unless it's necessary for a physical reason. When you lie down, your energy tends to dissipate along the spine. When you sit upright, energy flows upward, creating a more focused state of attention.

It's best to wait at least two hours after a meal before meditating. It's difficult for the body to fully attend to digestion and meditation at the same time. Your energy will be divided in two opposing directions. The meditation may suffer from drowsiness, or digestion might be hampered (even to the point of feeling queasy).

Seated Postures for Meditation

Now you're ready to sit. Find a posture that reflects the inner strength and calm that is your objective. Sit in a comfortable cross-legged position,[16] or back on the heels (toes together, heels separated to the side), or in a chair with the soles of your feet flat on the floor.

Have your head erect (chin parallel to the floor). The spine is upright with the chest expanded, but relaxed. It's best not to have the weight of your torso on the tailbone and sacrum. Instead, the weight

---

[16] There are a number of wonderful cross-legged postures that can be found in a good Hatha Yoga manual, but don't feel obliged to force your body to sit in a pose that requires great flexibility. A simple cross-legged position is perfectly fine. No one became enlightened because of how they sat.

BUILDING BLOCKS FOR SUCCESS IN MEDITATION

should be shifted to the sitz bones. The "sitz bones" is the nickname for the ischial tuberosities. They are the lowest of the three major bones that make up the pelvis. They're part of the pelvic girdle that supports the body when we sit. To make sure that your weight is on the sitz bones, lean forward slightly, arching the lower back a little bit. You will feel yourself rolling over the sitz bones. As you come back up to an erect posture, adjust it so that the sitz bones take the entire weight of the upper body. This frees the spine and makes upright sitting more comfortable. Don't get too "anatomical" about this. Thinking only of bones and spines is not the best approach. Use it as a starting point. Pay attention to how you feel and make adjustments until you are balanced, stable, and comfortable. Do the same even if you meditate sitting on a chair.

The hands can be folded in front of you or the palms can be face up or down on the knees with forefinger and thumb touching and the other three fingers open and relaxed.[17]

Make a firm resolve that you will allow the body to be perfectly still for the duration of your sitting. Every cell in our body is ready to obey your instructions if they are clear and strong.

The eyes can be closed or half-open, if that's natural for you. Make sure there is no tension around them. The eyes are closely connected to the ability to focus. Tension around the eyes tends to bring tension to the mind. Feel that your eyes are gentle and soft.

Take a quick mental inventory of your body. As you scan it, let go of any tension you find. Give the tense body part the instruction, "Relax." A stressed body will tend to create tension in the mind. A relaxed body will help calm the mind.

If, after sitting for a while you find that you are experiencing discomfort that repeatedly disturbs your focus on the object of meditation, gently adjust your posture. You don't want to spend your time meditating on pain. You can extend your legs for a few moments

---

[17] This hand position or *mudra* is called *chin mudra*, the sign or seal of wisdom. The forefinger and thumb represent the individual and the Absolute, respectively. The individual leaves the other three fingers (symbolizing attachments to worldly affairs) and reaches for union with the Absolute. But the index finger cannot touch the thumb unless the thumb also reaches toward the index finger. Sometimes, in our zeal to know God, we forget that God is also reaching for us. The touching of the thumb and forefinger also connects subtle energy circuits that are conducive to meditation. There are other hand mudras for meditation, but this is probably the most widely used.

See *mudra* in the *Sanskrit Glossary*.

if necessary. Even if you have to move, try not to disturb the meditative mood. Keep the awareness within. Little by little you will gain mastery over the meditative posture you have chosen.

BREATHING PRACTICES

Pranayama is one of the most important practices in Yoga. Usually translated as breath control, the term is composed of two words, *prana* (life force) + *ayama* (to regulate or control). The word's roots suggest that pranayama is not primarily about breathing to oxygenate the body. Pranayama's benefits to the body and mind result from increasing your stock of prana and regulating it so that it pulsates rhythmically and strongly throughout your system.

Prana is the vital energy present everywhere in creation. All movement, from the rotation of planets, to our voluntary and involuntary movements, to the subtlest movements within the atom, is an expression of prana.

Our bodies require prana to function. We can live for weeks without food, days without water, and minutes without oxygen, but if prana leaves, the body instantly ceases to exist. Good health and abundant energy are the result of the proper supply and distribution of prana in our systems.

The benefits of pranayama are many. Physically, it energizes the body, removes toxins, and strengthens the subtle and gross nervous systems.

Mentally, pranayama helps de-stress and focus the mind. If our supply of prana is low, or its movements irregular, our thoughts will be hazy, restless, scattered, and confused. Strong, rhythmic pulsations of prana lead to clear, orderly thoughts. If the prana in our system is abundant and rhythmic, we will have attained a perfect preparatory state for meditation. That is why pranayama is included in the meditation routine.

We get prana from food, breathing, and from positive, selfless, loving thoughts and actions. The following suggestions help maximize your supply of prana, while minimizing its wastage.
- Practice pranayama daily as part of a Hatha Yoga routine and as a preparation for meditation.
- A pure vegetarian diet supplies abundant prana, and requires less prana than meat to digest. You can achieve success in meditation if you eat meat, but it's easier if you don't.[18]

---

[18] See the chapter on the *Diet* for more information.

- Have speech that is tranquil, truthful, pleasant, and beneficial.
- Cultivate compassionate thoughts and actions.
- Be mindful of what you do for recreation. Some activities mostly drain energy. Note the effects of your choices for rest and relaxation and adjust accordingly. Experiment with uplifting books, sacred texts, and music, movies, TV shows, and art that inspire, energize, and inform you.

Three Fundamental Techniques

Now that you've explored the basics of prana and pranayama, you're ready to practice three fundamental breathing techniques, *deergha swasam*, the three-part deep breath, *nadi suddhi*, the alternate nostril breath, and *kapalabhati*, rapid diaphragmatic breathing. For the best results, do them in this order, two or three times a day.

All the inhalations and exhalations in these practices are through the nose.

Never strain when doing any pranayama practice. They are very powerful. If you ever even feel a little dizzy, lightheaded, or tingly, immediately discontinue the practice until the feeling completely passes.

Deergha Swasam

Deergha swasam is the fundamental breathing practice and uses the full capacity of the lungs. However, it is more important to have a controlled, easy breath than a deep one. The breathing is quiet. Ideally, if someone is sitting next to you, they won't hear you breathing.
- Sit comfortably with the spine erect, but not stiff. Shoulders are back with the chest well spread and the chin parallel to the floor. Eyes are closed. Hands are palms down on the knees to help steady the posture.
- Bring your awareness to the breathing. Just watch it for a few moments. Tune into its flow and rhythm.
- Exhale completely through the nose.
- At the end of the exhalation, pull in on the abdomen a little to squeeze out more air from the lungs.
- Begin the inhalation by allowing the abdomen to relax. Continue to inhale, expanding the abdomen as if it were a balloon filling with air.

- When the abdomen is completely expanded, breathe in more, feeling the ribcage expand.
- When the ribcage has expanded fully, inhale a little more. See if you can feel the collarbones rise a bit.
- Exhale in the opposite order than you inhaled. Allow the collarbones to lower, then the ribcage, and finally the abdomen.
- At the end of the exhalation, pull in on the abdomen a little. Begin the next round with an inhalation.

Repeat five times. You can add one breath a week until you reach ten as long as you avoid any strain. If you would like to progress beyond ten breaths, please seek out personal instruction.

Kapalabhati

Kapalabhati, literally, "skull shining breath," is rapid diaphragmatic breathing (that's why it's also referred to as the bellows breath). It awakens the body and mind and releases toxins. Kapalabhati is especially good for cleansing the subtle nerve currents in the head and moving energy upward. Its name recalls the shaved heads of yogis in India who would find their skulls shining with a light coat of perspiration after performing a few rounds.

- Sit comfortably, with the hands palm down on the knees.
- Exhale completely. At the end of the exhalation, pull in on the abdomen a bit.
- Inhale, let the abdomen expand to about half capacity.
- To exhale, quickly snap in on the abdominal muscles. This will force the air out of the lungs. This breath is not quiet, as it is with deergha swasam and nadi suddhi. You should hear the whoosh of air coming out through the nose.
- Release the abdomen and the air will come back in automatically. There is no effort on the inhalation.
- Continue for 15 expulsions.
- On the final expulsion, pull in on the abdomen a little more.
- Inhale deeply, using deergha swasam.
- Slowly exhale and return the breathing to normal.

This constitutes one round. Try doing three rounds of fifteen expulsions to start. Over time, you can increase the number of expulsions to one hundred and the number of rounds to five. Please keep in mind that this is a vigorous practice. Those with hypertension, headaches, abdominal disorders, or other such problems should seek the counsel of a physician before starting this practice and an experienced Yoga instructor for personal guidance.

Nadi Suddhi

Nadi suddhi is alternate nostril breathing. It incorporates deergha swasam with switching nostrils with each breath.
- Check your posture as above.
- Make a gentle fist with the right hand. The left hand remains palm down on the knee.
- Bring the right hand up to the nose. The upper arm should be relaxed at your side.
- Extend the thumb, ring, and pinky fingers. There's no need to stretch them out. Just release them from the fist.
- Exhale through both nostrils.
- Close off the right nostril with the thumb, and inhale through the left. To close the nostril, press on the side of the nostril rather than block it with the thumb.
- Press closed the side of the left nostril with the last two fingers, release the thumb, and exhale through the right nostril.
- Inhale through the right nostril.
- Close the right nostril and exhale through the left.
- This constitutes one full round.

Continue, remembering that the sequence is to inhale, close, switch, and exhale. The breathing should be rhythmic and quiet. You can count, "OM one, OM two," etc., to help keep the pace steady.

Once you are comfortable with the routine of alternating nostrils, you can increase the benefits of this practice by gradually prolonging the duration of the exhalation until it is twice as long as the inhalation. For example, if you can comfortably inhale for a count of three, exhale for six. Try to perform five rounds at the two-to-one ratio. Remember, it is important that you never strain.

You can gently increase the count by one for the inhalation and two for the exhalation every week or two until you reach a count of ten for the inhalation and twenty for the exhalation.[19] You can also gradually increase the number of rounds to ten per sitting.

---

[19] Don't rush the increase in count. It's fine if you progress more slowly. What's important is to make sure that you are comfortable at each stage.

BUILDING BLOCKS FOR SUCCESS IN MEDITATION

Breath Retention

Breath retention is an important and beneficial aspect of pranayama, but it is one that should be approached with great care. Even a little strain can cause physical harm and increase the restlessness of the mind. The body must be strengthened and the subtle nerve pathways purified before beginning the practice. It is best to seek the advice of a senior teacher before attempting breath retention.

AFFIRMATIONS, CHANTS, PRAYERS

A good meditation routine will gently, but surely coax the mind inward.[20] Let's review what we've covered so far:
- A steady, comfortable posture helped us move beyond body consciousness.
- We shifted our attention to the breath, the link between the body and mind to regulate and tune into the subtle, powerful flows and rhythms of the prana within.

Now we are ready to go more deeply inward, to the mind. To do this we turn to affirmations, chants, and prayers to generate clear intention and focused attention. We remind ourselves of our purpose in meditating and rouse the heart energy, the greatest storehouse of vitality we have. When that energy is stirred, the mind receives a turbocharged boost of prana. This is important, since meditation, which outwardly seems so still and calm, requires a great mobilization of inner resources.

You can use prayers, affirmations, and chants from any faith tradition, or you can create a mix from several traditions. Compose your own if you are moved to. Anything that's meaningful will work.

This part of the meditation routine can be very rewarding and enjoyable. Experiment to find what works for you. You can change, expand, or even reduce what you include according to what's happening in your life at any given time and your inner promptings.

The sample meditation routines presented later in this book, offer some examples of affirmations, chants, and prayers from the yogic tradition.

---

[20] For more experienced meditators: Every so often, there may be occasions when the meditative mood is particularly strong. The mind, for whatever reason, is already clear and calm and is drawn within. At those times, the preparatory practices can actually be a distraction. The meditative mood is important enough that you can skip some or all the preparation and just meditate. You can add the missing elements later.

BUILDING BLOCKS FOR SUCCESS IN MEDITATION

THE GOLDEN MOMENT

There is one more step to take before turning your attention to the object of meditation. It's simple and doesn't take long, but it is vital.

These are the two periods of time in a meditation session where you create an inner environment that is nonjudgmental, accepting, gentle, and loving. During this stage, we allow whatever comes into our awareness to rise, develop, and subside without any interference or judgment. The Golden Moment is the loving acceptance of the entire mindscape – the thoughts, images, impressions, emotions, memories, and activities that constitute our minds at any given moment. It is a meditation essential and a gift we give ourselves, a gift that leads to peace of mind, wisdom, and unconditional love.

Why the Golden Moment is Important

The biggest reason that people are irregular in their practice, or drop it completely, is that they don't feel that they've experienced enough benefits. A major cause for this failure is the mental environment that they have allowed to exist in meditation.

For many practitioners, meditating resembles warfare. The chosen object of meditation is like an embattled victim being showered by bombs while running through a minefield. The distracting thoughts are regarded as enemies of meditation. This attitude sets up a combative and tense mental environment, where only the chosen object of meditation is "good" and everything else is "bad." It's hard *not* to feel inadequate or like a failure. Cultivating the Golden Moment neutralizes this nonproductive attitude.

How it's Done

You simply remain a silent witness to the mind, without making any judgment as to the fitness of its contents. There is no attempt to control, guide, or censor mental activities. You simply observe, allowing impressions to move across the stage that is your awareness. Like a member of the audience – not like a critic – you simply watch.

The Golden Moment regards the mental activity in meditation as typical and nonpathological. Its practice leads to accepting all thoughts and activities with compassion and love, a profound and complete embrace of our mindscape.

When it's Practiced

The Golden Moment is practiced just before turning the awareness to the object of meditation and again, at the end before the closing peace chants.

Why Two Golden Moments

The Golden Moment at the beginning helps calm and clear the mind, preparing it to embrace the chosen object of meditation easily and comfortably. It creates a more hospitable environment for meditation to take root and grow. From the outset of your sitting, you've let go of the tension that accompanies notions of success and failure, or of good and bad thoughts. The subtle and powerful energies of the mind become freer to focus.

The second Golden Moment reestablishes the nonjudgmental attitude if it is lost while meditating and helps to integrate the meditative experience with the more active, get-things-done part of the mind.

As you progress over time, this second session takes on another significant dimension. A mind that is no longer threatened by critical judgments, more easily reveals subtler states of consciousness. There is a natural deepening of awareness from the object of meditation, to the peace within, to awareness of awareness, and ultimately to the experience of Self-realization.

How Long

The time you spend practicing the Golden Moment can range from several moments to several minutes. It depends on how long your meditation session is and the state of your mind at any given time.

The first Golden Moment should be continued until the mind begins to become clearer and calmer. Then, move on to the chosen object of meditation.

The second Golden Moment can be done for as long as you like, or until the mind starts to lose focus.

Don't rush or skimp on this aspect of your practice. Cultivating the Golden Moment will accelerate your success.

Please see *Intention, Attention, and Nonjudgmental Attitude*, for more on the nonjudgmental attitude that constitutes the Golden Moment.

HOW TO END A SESSION

It's important to integrate the benefits of meditation into your day. Although this needn't take long, don't skip or scamper through it. Here's a good three-step guideline:
- After the Golden Moment, take two or three easy, deep breaths.
- Dedicate the fruits of your practice for the welfare of others by offering thoughts or prayers for their peace and well-being. Include all of creation: people, animals, plants – everything. Don't leave out anyone, especially someone you have hard feelings towards. These few minutes give you the opportunity to open your heart to lovingkindness and compassion.
- Gratefully acknowledge your guru or teachers, and the form of God you are devoted to. The simple act of grateful remembrance of those that have guided and supported you fosters humility and keeps the mind open to the continued guidance needed to experience the highest peace.

There will be times when your meditation was not too focused or peaceful. You can redeem it with a proper ending. Be attentive to the words and meaning of your affirmations and prayers. Envision what you are saying.

You've now completed the meditation session, but don't get up abruptly like toast popping out of a toaster. Sit for a few moments, and notice how you feel. No matter how your session felt to you, you succeeded in doing something great. Even if it doesn't seem like it, you've achieved some mastery over the mind. You are on the same road tread by all enlightened beings. They started just like you.

DEVELOP A SENSIBLE PRACTICE

How Often to Meditate

To experience the best of what meditation has to offer, daily meditation is essential. Sit twice a day, every day. Once a day is still fantastic.

If that seems too daunting, scale it back. Maybe resolve to meditate once or twice a day, four or five days a week. Pick your days, but don't be rigid. If you convince yourself that there is only one right way, only one way to success, you will have multiplied the options for failure. Daily meditation is best, semi-regular is still useful, occasional is better than nothing, but never meditating doesn't help at all.

Make a decision and stick to it. You can always adjust one way or the other over time. Just avoid being wishy-washy.

When to Meditate

The best times to meditate are first thing in the morning, noon, and at dusk or before retiring for the night.

Meditation's benefits are enhanced by early morning sittings. The mind is a fresh slate, and whatever you think reaches deeply into the subconscious. Predawn is also charged with an abundance, or prana, a wonderful healing tonic.

Traditionally, yogis have valued *brahmamuhurta*, the two hours before sunrise as the best time to meditate. The idea of getting up before sunrise can be intimidating at first, but it's well worth it. Why not try it on a few weekend days? See what it's like to be awake when the world is dark and quiet. Since your daily activities are several hours away, the mind doesn't tend to be occupied with thoughts of work and family.

If you can make a little time in the midst of your busy schedule, a noontime meditation is a boon. There is no better break, reliever of stress, and better preparation for the rest of the day.

Dusk is another good time to sit. Like dawn, dusk carries a natural stillness with it. Both times are junctures in the day that represent a shift of intentions: preparing to launch into the day's tasks, or getting ready to settle down for the evening.

Meditating before bedtime allows the stresses of the day to drain away, and can be an aid in experiencing better sleep. Meditation does energize some people, making sleep difficult. If you are in the latter category, there's no harm in sitting earlier in the evening. However, it's still worthwhile repeating peace chants or prayers before retiring for the night. To begin and end each day on a positive note creates momentum in your practice.

Find a Practical Time Slot

When you schedule daily meditations, arrange the time slot to be longer than the session itself. That way you won't feel rushed. If your sitting goes a couple of minutes longer, or you just wish to sit and enjoy the post-meditation peace, you have the time to do so.

When choosing a time to meditate, think through the scheduling details. For example, you decide that you will meditate for thirty minutes every morning. You leave for work at eight. It takes thirty minutes for your morning shower routine, and another thirty minutes for breakfast and to get dressed, so you have been setting your alarm for seven. If you reset it to go off at six-thirty to accommodate meditation, you are not leaving yourself any leeway. This tight schedule might cause anxiety. Even a minor delay might tempt you to skip your sitting or cut it short. Or you might spend your time concerned that you'll meditate too long, or thinking about the day's upcoming activities.

Instead of getting up at six-thirty, try six-fifteen. The extra fifteen minutes can make the difference between a harried morning with a stressed meditation, and a pleasant, productive one that becomes the ideal way to start the day.

How Long to Meditate

For most beginners, two sittings of twenty minutes is a great place to start. The twenty minutes includes chants, affirmations, breathing practices, the silent meditation period, and closing chants. A rule of thumb is that the preparatory segment should be about one-quarter to one-third the length of your session (don't get rigid with this – it's a guideline). This applies even if your sitting is one hour long. If you're meditating longer than that on a regular basis, you probably don't need further advice. Just be careful not to overdo it. The mind can become fatigued, and what seems like a wonderful, sage-like sitting can be mostly lounging in a half-sleep state.

How and When to Increase the Length of Your Meditation

This is not just a matter of resetting your meditation timer. Determining how long to meditate requires clarity of purpose and a realistic evaluation of how much time and energy you're willing and able to commit to practice. Assess what value the practice holds for you, your goals, and your limitations.

Be aware that new meditators are often victims of being overly enthusiastic. Their eagerness to succeed causes them to set unrealistic goals. A goal of meditating two hours every sitting may sound grand. We may think that we'll attain the fruits of meditation quicker. It doesn't usually work that way. Experience should remind us of the fate of most dramatic resolves. We're usually fine for a few days or weeks. After that, our resolve slips away and we return to our old habits.

Setting unrealistic goals can be a trick of the ego. When goals are beyond our reach, we inevitably fail, allowing the ego to return to its old habits. To make matters worse, the failure to live up to our goals reinforces thoughts regarding our own inadequacy. Be honest with yourself and reflect on the advice of experienced meditators who counsel moderation. Your goals should prompt you to stretch, not strain.

If you are content and growing with two sittings of twenty minutes each, there's no need to change. Continue with this routine as long as you are enjoying it and your meditations are growing in peace, clarity, and focus. However, if you've been feeling that the meditations are too brief and that you might benefit from longer sessions, you may be ready to explore lengthening your sittings.

Try increasing from two twenty-minute sessions to two thirty-minute sessions every day, or sit for thirty minutes in the morning and twenty in the evening.

Continue with your new timing for a few weeks to confirm your feelings. You can gradually increase the length of your sessions until they are an hour long. An hour sitting is long enough to achieve and sustain deep meditative states. If you wish to sit longer than that on a regular basis, seek the advice of an experienced teacher.

You don't have to increase both daily sittings to an hour. You can build a wonderful practice with an hour sitting in the morning and a

BUILDING BLOCKS FOR SUCCESS IN MEDITATION

half-hour in the evening. If you have the zeal and time, add a noon meditation.

Continue to educate yourself on the benefits of a regular meditation practice. Affirm that success is assured if you persevere. Meditation is a science. If you practice it faithfully and reasonably, you *will* see the results.

How to Time Your Meditation Session

It's a common question: *If I'm supposed to be focused on the object of meditation, how do I keep track of time?* You could make a firm resolve that you will meditate until a certain hour. There is a part of the brain that subconsciously keeps track of time. This is not realistic for most. The simpler solution is to buy an oven or egg timer. Find one that isn't startling. There are even applications for smart phones that are designed to time meditations. Set the alarm and forget about the time. Focus on meditating.

If you are repeating a mantra, use of mala beads can be helpful for timing.

THE DISTRACTED MIND SYNDROME

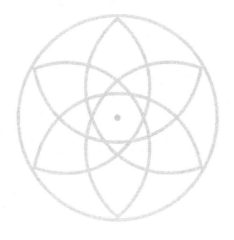

WHAT HAPPENS WHEN THE MIND SHAKES

This chapter is about the challenges that practitioners face when meditating and about other areas of life that affect progress in meditation.

The following list is from the *Yoga Sutras of Patanjali*. Every seeker faces these obstacles at some point on their spiritual journey.

1.30. Disease, dullness, doubt, carelessness, laziness, sensuality, false perception, failure to reach firm ground, and slipping from the ground gained—these distractions of the mind-stuff are the obstacles.

The words translated as distraction are *chitta vikshepa*. Chitta is the mind. Vikshepa means false projection, dispersing, and shaking. These obstacles are symptoms of a lack or loss of focus and intention, an unsteadiness or shaking of awareness. They are the polar opposite of the clarity and steady focus of a mind in meditation. They form a chain reaction, one leading to the next.

Disease. This stands for *dis*-ease, any physical discomfort or disorder that prevents us from fully engaging in meditation or other spiritual practices. It can present in many ways, including fatigue, an aching lower back, nagging allergies, or headaches. Some of these symptoms may mostly appear just before or during meditation. Regardless of the specifics, practice becomes irregular due to physical discomfort.

Dullness. The result of irregular practice is that not much progress is made. It's hard to stay inspired if you don't experience anything nice in your meditation. The mind begins to have a hard time focusing. A dull mind lacks insight and can't penetrate into deeper realities. You feel that your meditations are stagnating. A still, focused mind begins to seem like an impossible dream.

The next stage naturally follows...

Doubt. *"I don't know. Meditation makes extreme demands. It seems too rigid or idealistic. Maybe I don't have the talent for this. I'm starting to wonder if meditation is for me."*

We doubt the truth or practicality of the teachings, or even more troublesome, we doubt ourselves. We haven't made the progress we thought we would. We feel a bit let down. Our hearts are no longer in our practice.

THE DISTRACTED MIND SYNDROME

Doubt can be a serious impediment to progress. It hampers discrimination, fills the mind with questions that seem to have no answer, and brings up uncertainties regarding our self-worth.

When practice has stalled due to doubt, have the doubts cleared. Ask questions of experienced teachers, read and study more, do whatever it takes to address the uncertainties.

Doubt, along with being its own difficulty, adds fuel to dullness.

Carelessness. Even though the first three obstacles are working their spell, you persevere, but without much enthusiasm. Your practice becomes mechanical and lacks conviction and healthy intensity.

The mind, torn by doubt and its energy dissipated by disease and dullness, is prone to carelessness. The end of your meditation session arrives and you have no idea what you have been doing for the past thirty minutes. It probably *wasn't* repeating your mantra.

You cease making progress and begin to lose momentum.

Laziness. Meditation practice now becomes nothing more than a chore. Do you feel like meditating? Not likely. You become neglectful regarding your practice. If we do not even attempt to better ourselves, how can there be hope for success?

Sensuality. The mind now becomes bored with meditation, and a bored mind looks for distraction, a new amusement, something else to do. It gets mischievous. If it cannot find satisfaction in meditation, it will look to gratify the senses.

The Sanskrit word translated as sensuality, *avirati*, means "to dissipate" and refers to the dissipation of energy that comes when the mind loses its resolve and seeks to satisfy sensual cravings. Scattered energy exacerbates the other obstacles.

False perception. *"There are aspects of Yoga that are great, but some Eastern philosophies seem life denying. Isn't life to be enjoyed? I'm certainly not enjoying meditating. I'm thinking that meditation is really about the suppression of natural impulses and emotions."*

What seemed clearly true in the beginning is now questionable. We may begin to believe that our assessment of meditation as a meaningful part of our lives was a mistake. Most practices are abandoned, except for a few stress-relieving techniques.

Failure to reach firm ground. It is difficult to make progress when the practices have not become firmly grounded, an integral part of our lives. It's too easy to get sidetracked. Failure to reach firm ground is also the inability to attain focused attention.

Slipping from the ground gained. It can happen because you fall back into harmful habits, or into extended periods of physical or emotional stress; or even because after making a little progress, you become a little complacent and "rest on your laurels." Whatever the reason, it is a common experience to temporarily lose some of the progress you've made.

It is very discouraging to work hard, make some progress, and then slip back. It can feel like Dante's vision of hell, where poor souls expend tremendous energy to crawl out of an immense, burning pit only to fall back into the flames at the brink of escape.

Prescription for a Shaky Mind

Yoga offers a powerful treatment strategy to overcome the obstacles created by a shaky mind. It begins with our attitude toward them. They are not enemies to attack. There's no stress or fear when they're encountered because we can learn valuable lessons from them.

As obstacles appear, we rightly treat them as teachers that uncover hidden weaknesses and strengths. Unseen weaknesses work mischief in the subconscious, silently impelling us to actions or reactions we find unpleasant or harmful. Meanwhile, strengths that remain tucked away from consciousness are left partially developed. When obstacles come creeping (or sometimes erupting) from their subconscious caves, we can effectively deal with them.

The *Yoga Sutras* present a two-part prescription for overcoming obstacles: a remedy for times when they are active, and a preventive that inoculates us from future attacks. These principles, along with the benefits of the company of like-minded seekers (*satsang*), and of selfless service, are all we need to continue progressing.

The remedy. *From this practice (referring to mantra repetition), the awareness turns inward, and the distracting obstacles vanish.* 1.29.

Although the text presents mantra repetition as the cure, we can by extension, include any regular meditation practice.

Obstacles are not overcome by forceful efforts to push them away. That only strengthens them. They crave attention and thrive on it. Deprive them of attention by repeatedly refocusing on the object of meditation, and they gradually whither.

THE DISTRACTED MIND SYNDROME

The preventive. *The concentration on a single subject (or the use of one technique) is the best way to prevent the obstacles and their accompaniments.* 1.32.

Commitment is the preventive against future occurrences of the obstacles. Steadiness of mind is the basis for both courses of treatment, with focused attention in meditation as the remedy and perseverance as the preventive.

There is a story that demonstrates the power of sticking to one thing. It begins with a young boy's first day of school.

Students, today is special: your first day of school. We will treat this day as a holiday. I'll send you home early, after teaching you something that you can show your parents. We will learn to write the number one.

The class was thrilled. The teacher turned to the blackboard and traced the single stroke for the class to see and practice.

One by one, she checked all the students' papers.

Good. Fine. Very nice. You have all done very well. You are dismissed for today.

The next day, the teacher gave a new assignment.

Boys and girls, we can continue to number two.

She drew the number on the board. Again, she strolled up and down the isles checking the papers. Then she came to one boy who seemed to have misunderstood the assignment . . .

Son, you are still writing number one. Today we are practicing number two. Your number ones are fine, please move on.

Teacher, I know we are doing number two, but somehow I feel that I don't understand the number one yet.

Well...OK. I'll let you continue with it today, but you must catch up with the class by tomorrow or you will fall too far behind.

The next day the teacher wrote the number three on the board, but our hero was still practicing the number one.

O, son, you are still practicing number one! Your number one is perfectly acceptable. There is no reason for you to continue practicing it.

I understand, teacher. I don't want to cause any trouble; it's just that I don't feel I understand the number one.

Days passed and the class continued to advance, while our young man insisted on practicing number one. Finally, in a moment of great exasperation, the teacher lost her temper.

Go home. I'm at my wit's end. Maybe your parents can do something with you.

The boy went home and explained what happened to his parents. They were shaken. They hoped that they could guide him through this perplexing problem, but the boy continued the same behavior. Everyday they made their best effort and everyday he replied...

I am sorry to hurt you. I don't mean to disobey; it is just that I don't understand the number one.

After a few weeks of this, even his parents lost their temper.

You're so stubborn. Leave us alone. Get out of our sight.

Quietly the boy left, entering the forest at the edge of their village. Moments later, the parents, regretting their outburst, searched for their son, but could not find him.

Weeks passed, until one day the boy appeared at the classroom. The teacher, excited, yet restrained by the boy's past behavior, simply welcomed him and then added...

Is there anything we can do for you son?

Teacher, I know the number one.

Would you like to come up to the front of the room and show everyone your number one?

Certainly, if you like.

The little boy calmly walked to the front of the room. Picking up the chalk and turning to the blackboard, he traced the simple straight line of the number one . . . and the blackboard *split in half*.

The boy's focused attention on writing the number one resulted in an extraordinary demonstration of the power of a one-pointed mind. His simple act took on miraculous dimensions.

He intuitively realized that his *awareness* in writing the number one and the *physical act* of writing it were not unified. He persisted until his mind was fully united with the act. His intentions, thoughts, and actions became fully integrated.[21]

We need that kind of one-pointed perseverance to overcome obstacles and pierce the veneer of ignorance. Keep in mind that anyone who has achieved mastery has devoted a great deal of time and effort to overcoming challenges. No accomplished athlete, musician, or cabinetmaker ever succeeded without finding ways of prevailing over obstacles. Meditation is not different. It is a process, not an event.

We should never give up. Many people quit when they are on the brink of success. Perseverance always pays off. Ants, daily walking the same path across a stone wall, will wear a groove in it one day. Likewise, our practices will eventually eradicate ignorance.

---

[21] Noteworthy was his perseverance in the face of challenges. He continued on his quest despite the advice of an expert (his teacher) and his parents.

MORE OBSTACLES

If your meditation isn't progressing as well as you hoped, look here. This list addresses obstacles that might not seem connected to meditation practice. Though they may not directly relate to technique, they are major factors in determining success or failure in meditation – and happiness or unhappiness in life. They focus on habits, values, personal environment, and self-image.

Self-deception

This obstacle is pervasive. Our strong tendency is to think of ourselves not as we *are*, but how we *wish* we were. Without a clear idea of what our strengths and weaknesses are, we can't grow. Some individuals try to convince themselves that they want to meditate, but it's a wish that doesn't run too deep. They begin meditating because their friends do it, they saw it on TV, or they're searching for a "cure" for the suffering in their lives. In truth, they're not really ready to give it a sincere try.

Be honest with yourself. If you only have a slight interest in meditating, keep your goals simple and light. From honest, humble beginnings great practices can grow.

Gossip and Backbiting

Gossip and backbiting drain us of energy. No one feels uplifted after bad-mouthing someone or even listening to someone being denigrated.

Skeptics

Honest, reasoned, skepticism has important benefits. We can learn from skeptics. They can nudge us to take a fresh and deeper look at our beliefs and actions. Be open to such criticism. On the other hand, be wary of people who are intent on being negative or making light of your interest in meditation. It can shake your faith in the practice.

Negative Work Environment

Living or working in a negative environment where unethical, immoral, or illegal behavior, intolerance, violence, or selfishness is prominent can be a real impediment to peace of mind. A negative environment brings subtle, corrosive influences into the conscious and subconscious mind.

Disturbing Entertainment

Violent movies, music with violent lyrics, entertainment that denigrates a person, race, faith tradition, lifestyle, sexual preference, or nationality can reinforce patterns of thought that are not favorable to positive states of mind. Be mindful of how these diversions affect your mind and stay away from those that disturb you.

Overwork

Hard work is healthy. Overwork tires the body and mind, making meditation difficult.

Jealousy

Know that you are given exactly what you need at every moment. Nothing is lacking for you to grow and learn. Keep your attention on what's on your side of the fence and make the best out of what you are given. You will find hidden gems.

Unchecked or Unexamined Desires

Freedom does not lie in following impulses. True freedom is a mind that focuses on what brings benefit, not solely on what it *feels* like doing.

Not Living According to Your Values

There is a part of the mind that monitors integrity. Consciously or unconsciously, we get high grades for having our beliefs, words, and actions in accord. On the other hand, our self-image suffers when we fail to live up to the standards we endorse.

Lack of Selfless Service

Meditation is tested and strengthened by a life dedicated to the welfare of others.[22]

---

[22] See the chapter on *Karma Yoga*.

Arrogance

This unpleasant trait can pop up almost any time. It can begin by feeling that we are right about something. A need to validate ourselves, to be correct or seen as correct, often overshadows reason and fact. If we convince ourselves that our view is the correct one, we might temporarily prop up a chronically sagging self-image. In truth, arrogant people – skilled, knowledgeable, or not – are lacking self-esteem. The shame of it is that they end up pushing people away from them and they miss some positive qualities that they do possess. Humility keeps the mind open, supple, and quick.

Adrenalin Addiction

We often misinterpret a nervous system that's shifted into overdrive as happiness. Adrenalin rushes into the bloodstream, the heart rate increases, and blood pressure rises. It's part of the fight or flight response. Stirred from complacency or the boredom of routine, we feel more alive, powerful, and alert. Don't mistake excitement, even if from a positive source, as the happiness rooted in the Self. The happiness we seek is complete, balanced, and unshakable. It has no opposite. It is the happiness beyond happiness, beyond words.

Complacency

When the mind gains a little focus in meditation, you may experience an elevated happiness, something you've never known before. You feel that you've made some real progress. You have made progress, but don't let the mind get attached to it. The highest states usually aren't experienced right away. Don't settle for a taste of happiness. Successful meditators don't compromise their goals. They continue their journey until suffering is transcended. Don't get stuck in nice, when wonderstruck is available.

Boredom

We love change. We've become conditioned to respond favorably to something new and different. We eagerly look for the latest cell phone, TV, or fashion. Some even become bored with their life partners. Learn to appreciate the variety that comes with going deep with one thing, rather than constantly looking for something else. As we go deeper in meditation, new vistas on life appear, and new

THE DISTRACTED MIND SYNDROME

insights into who we are manifest.

Irregular Practice

The mind that wanders from the object of meditation within a sitting, and the mind that wanders from daily practice are both symptoms of the same obstacle: unsteadiness of mind.

Falling Asleep
- To try to avoid dozing off, consider the following hints:
- Get adequate sleep at night.
- Don't eat for at least two hours before meditating. Meditating on a light or empty stomach is best.
- Take a cool shower before you meditate.
- Do some jumping jacks or other aerobic exercise.
- Don't meditate in a room that is too warm or cover yourself up with too many blankets. If you're too warm, you will likely feel drowsy.
- Be sure to do breathing practices to awaken the mind. Bellows breathing (kapalabhati) is especially useful.
- If you are using a mantra, you can repeat it out loud, or silently with lip movement. Use of a mala (rosary) will help keep you alert. Should you begin to doze off, the first thing that happens is your arm will drop and wake you up.[23]
- Group meditations can help keep you alert. It's embarrassing to be the only person in the room snoring.
- If all else fails, try meditating while standing. It's certainly not the best posture for meditation, but it's important to break the habit of sleep before it gets too ingrained.

---

[23] See *mala* in the *Sanskrit Glossary*.

EXPERIENCES IN MEDITATION

In meditation you will experience peace, contentment, inner harmony, and an integration of all aspects of your being. Insights into your self and the nature of life may emerge. These are the true gems of meditation.

Other meditation experiences are more "mystical." These flashier experiences can be indicators of progress, or the product of imagination or of subconscious desires to experience something out of the ordinary. Though they may be pleasurable, they are not the most reliable gauges of success. The most dependable way to assess progress is to note if you are becoming more peaceful, patient, cheerful, loving, thoughtful, and courageous. Daily life is the lab where meditation is tested and refined.

Regardless of what you experience within a meditation session, treat every experience like a page in a novel. A page may include drama, wonders, intrigue, or inspiration. It could just as well be boring, commonplace, unsettling, or annoying. Regardless, you don't usually read a page over and over. No single page defines the story. We turn the page so that the story can progress. Similarly, don't dwell on any experience in meditation. No matter how entrancing, disconcerting, or uneventful, turn the page. Tomorrow is another day.

Don't think of these experiences as a to-do list. It's not necessary to go through all of them. What we experience in meditation is determined by what we need to grow, our experiences in life, and the depth of our meditation. Each meditation is meaningful in its own way.

Lights

You might see various colors and shapes of light. The colors are aspects of subtle matter. Every element has its own color. Dark, grey, or cloudy colors indicate that dullness of mind is predominating. Bright colors represent restless energy, and golden or white luminescent colors show that balance is dominant.[24] You might also have visions of light that look like the sun, moon, or stars. The light is within, now you are beginning to experience a little bit of it.

---

[24] These colors represent the three *gunas*: *tamas, rajas,* and *sattwa*. See the *Sanskrit Glossary* for details regarding the gunas in general, and each one specifically.

Feeling Weightless

A sensation of being very light or that you might begin to float. This is a sign that the prana is flowing upwards more strongly.

Energy Movements

Sometimes, you might feel movements of energy up the spine or like insects crawling on the body. These are movements of *prana*, opening up obstructions to the free flow of energy.

Sounds

You might hear sounds of various types: such as a bell, conch, cymbal, flute, drum, or thunder. These are manifestations of mantric vibrations within.

Divine Visions

You might have visions of deities or sages.

SAMPLE MEDITATION ROUTINES

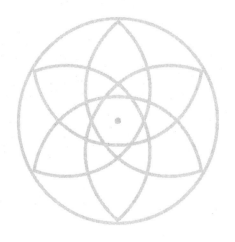

ROUTINE ONE
A Solid Foundation

The following routine presents a complete and balanced approach. It contains the essential elements of a good meditation session in a logical progression. It will give you a sense of how the different parts work together to encourage success. You can always add items, or delete or exchange those that ultimately don't work for you.

The rationale for the elements follows the routine.

Opening Chants[25]
OM OM OM

We all learn what we know from someone. No one is truly self-taught. We watch and listen; we emulate and question. The more open we are to guidance, the quicker and more certain our progress will be. The next chant, to the guru, is a way to cultivate receptivity, humility, and gratitude. While it can be done with thoughts of a particular guru in mind, it's ultimately about the nature of the Light that removes the darkness of ignorance.

OM *Namah Shivaya Gurave*
Satchidaanada Moorthaye
Nish Prapaanjaya Shaanthaya
Niraalambaya Tejase

The Guru is Auspiciousness, embodiment of Truth, Knowledge, Bliss
Salutations to the One who is beyond the worlds[26]
Peaceful Independent and Radiant

OM *Shanti Shanti Shanti*
OM *Peace, Peace, Peace*

---

[25] You can listen to an audio of these chants and more at: www.yogalifesociety.com

[26] Following is the most common list of the three worlds. They exist as realms, but more significantly, as aspects of every individual.
- *Bhuloka* = the material universe. It is the physical sphere.
- *Antarloka* = the subtle, astral plane. It is occupied by *devas* (divine beings). It is the mental and emotional sphere.
- *Brahmaloka* = the causal plane. Occupied by the gods and highly evolved souls. It is the superconscious sphere.
  Some list the three worlds as: *svarga* (heaven), *bhumi* (earth), and *patala* (the underworld).

SAMPLE MEDITATION ROUTINES

Pranayama
Deergha Swasam: three part deep breathing: 5-10 rounds
Kapalabhati: bellows breathing: 3 rounds of 15-50 expulsions per round, depending on your experience and physical condition
Nadi Suddhi: alternate nostril breathing: 5 rounds

Affirmation
This could include any short prayer or intention that opens your heart and reminds you of your goal. For example,

Peace is my True Nature. To experience this, I will be attentive to my object of meditation from the beginning to the end of this sitting. I dedicate the benefits of my practice to the welfare of all creation.

Golden Moment #1

Silent Meditation with Your Chosen Object
15 minutes

Golden Moment #2

Coming Out of Silent Meditation
Take two or three deep breaths.

Peace Chants
Repeat the following chants with a deep wish that perfect peace prevail everywhere.

Asato maa sat gamaya
Tamaso maa jyothir gamaya
Mrityor maa amritam gamaya

Lead us from unreal to Real
Lead us from darkness to Light
Lead us from the fear of death to the knowledge of Immortality

OM *Shanti Shanti Shanti*
OM *Peace Peace Peace*

Lokaa Samastaa Sukino Bhavantu

May the entire universe be filled with Peace, and Joy; Love and Light

Pay Respects to the Guru

Following is an affirmation in which the word *satguru* is translated as the light of truth (*sat* = truth; *guru* = remover of darkness).

Jay Sri Satguru Maharaj Ki! Jai!
May the Light of Truth overcome all darkness! Victory to that Light!

SAMPLE MEDITATION ROUTINES

ROUTINE TWO
Drop Your Burdens

You can use this guided meditation, in whole or in part, for your regular routine or for an occasional change of pace. It can also be used for a group meditation.

Sometimes, even after years of practice, meditators feel that they haven't made enough progress. Their lack of success may be due to irregular practice, not dealing with the attachments that cause restlessness, or the inability to leave behind the day-to-day concerns that demand attention. This meditation focuses on the last cause.

With practice, you'll be able to drop these burdens by an act of will, without going through all the steps.

You can read the following script as written, or alter it according to your taste, temperament, and circumstances. If you are using it for a group meditation, give an overview of what will be happening and how long it will take (about 20 minutes, depending on what is included in the preparation and ending). Remind participants that there will be a period of silence (at least five minutes is recommended) during which they can use any meditation technique they are familiar with.[27]

Preparation
Chants, prayers, affirmations. Follow with pranayama.

Script
We are about to take a pilgrimage to a temple, a sacred space within you, where you can meet your True Self – the unshakable peace or God in you.

When you enter, all your cares, anxieties, and suffering will vanish. Your mind will be clear and focused; your heart joyful and carefree.

There is a requirement to enter. You need to drop your burdens. Leave all your worries and cares at the gate as you enter. Don't worry; they will be there as you exit. You can pick them up as you leave if you like.

To begin, sit comfortably with the spine erect, but not stiff. Gently close the eyes.

Bring your awareness to the breathing. Watch the natural flow and rhythm of the breath, without trying to control or affect it in any way. [Wait a minute or so before the next step.]

---

[27] There is an audio of this guided meditation. Please see www.yogalifesociety.com for details.

Now you are ready to turn your attention to the burdens that separate you from the peace that is your birthright.

Your financial concerns, let them go.

Your relationship problems. Place them outside the gateway.

To enter this sacred space you need to let go – at least temporarily – of being a mother, father, child, sister, or brother. You can resume these relationships later.

All the grudges you hold against others, let them go.

Worries over health – yours or your loved ones – drop them now. There is no need to worry over such matters here. You are completely safe and secure. No one or nothing can harm you.

If you have anxiety over your job, or lack of one, let it go.

Leave behind all your responsibilities. Right now, there is nothing that you need to do, worry over, or check up on. You have no responsibility other than to come face-to-face with the Peace that is your True Nature.

Let go of the feeling that others need you. The same Self that watches over you, cares for you, and guides you, is also with them.

You are alone, but not lonely.

Your failures. They are dead and gone. You have been carrying these guilt-ridden burdens for too long. Put them down.

The same with your successes, let them go.

Let go of being male or female; tall or short; slim or stocky; young or old. These things are not you, anyway. Let them go and be free.

Let go of wanting to be respected, admired, acknowledged, or even noticed. What heavy burdens they are!

Drop thoughts of good and bad; right and wrong; holy or unholy. You will be traveling beyond them all. The temple within is beyond dualities.

Leave behind all thoughts of past and future. In this moment, there are no memories, fears, or plans. There is only now, and that is sufficient.

Are there any other burdens that you hold? Take in a slow, deep breath...hold it for a few seconds...and as you slowly exhale, drop every last burden. Let them go, they bind you.

Finally, let go of any thoughts of what you will experience in this meditation. Be free of the fear of failure or the excitement of success. No expectations; no fear, just acceptance and peace.

Free of the burdens that have limited you, you are ready to go even deeper within.

With the clear, gentle focus of meditation, you can enter your inner temple.

Within, there is peace. You are home. Suffering vanishes. Here you discover that

SAMPLE MEDITATION ROUTINES

everything you have ever longed for, that you have prized – you are that and much more.

We'll begin a period of silent meditation now. Let the mind be calm and focused. Stay in the moment.

[Silent Meditation Period]

OM . . .

For the next few moments, rest in, and enjoy the peace, which is your True Nature.

With the following chants, send thoughts of healing, peace, and joy to one and all.

Asatho maa sat gamaya
Tamaso maa jyothir gamaya
Mrityor maa amritam gamaya

Lead us from unreal to Real
Lead us from darkness to the Light
Lead us from the fear of Death, to the knowledge of immortality

OM Shanthi Shanthi Shanthi
OM Peace Peace Peace

Lokaa Samastaa Sukhino Bhavanthu
May the entire Universe be filled with Peace and Joy; Love and Light.

May the Light of Truth Overcome All Darkness! Victory to that Light!
Jai Sri Satguru Maharaj Ki! Jai!

SUCCESS IS IN THE DETAILS: HINTS AND SUGGESTIONS THAT WORK

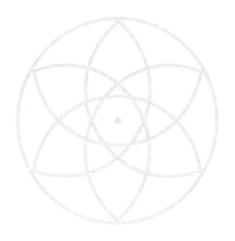

REGULARITY

Many people begin the practice of meditation with high hopes for success, only to give up after a few weeks or months. There are no revelations or mind-expanding visions. They see no bright lights or hear celestial sounds. They experience meditation as a struggle to calm a mind that is hell-bent on focusing on anything but the object of meditation. *It doesn't have to be that way.*

The real secret – and this is really it, the secret of secrets – is regularity. Regularity is important for both the colon and for meditation.

Regularity creates the opportunity for growth in clarity, insight, and serenity. Success is built on a one day-at-a-time, one meditation-session at-a-time, one step-at-a-time, approach. With consistent practice, new positive habits gradually replace old, unwanted ones. Habits sustained over time become character. As that happens, practice comes naturally and is a joy.

At this point, you might be thinking, *"It's a catch twenty-two. I need to be regular to develop regularity."* That's true enough. The good news is that yogis have over 5000 years worth of effective hints that help develop regularity. We'll discuss:
- Group Support
- Visualization of the Goal
- Study
- Prayer, Worship, and Ritual
- Environment

Group Support

Shared meditations can form a solid foundation for growth as a meditator. It helps keep you motivated. Many meditators find that their sittings are deeper and more peaceful when done with a group.

The support of like-minded seekers is invaluable. It may be the single most potent tool in the Yoga toolbox. Members of organizations such as Weight Watchers and Alcoholics Anonymous know the power of group support: success is most easily achieved in a program that includes associating with people who share your interest. Group energy and wisdom is greater than the sum of its parts. Members are continually nourished, guided, and inspired.

This marvelous quote from a great eighth century sage, Adi Shankaracharya, extols the highest benefit of keeping the proper company in spiritual life:

> *When you are in good company, you cannot be in bad company.*
> *If you're not in bad company, you don't fall into delusion.*
> *If you keep out of delusion, your mind becomes steady.*
> *If your mind is steady, you are liberated.*

All the benefits, including enlightenment, naturally come with good company. Friends and acquaintances, who regularly or at least semi-regularly meditate, serve as a natural encouragement for you to continue with your practice.

Visualize the Goal

Cultivate a clear image of your goal. Keep your intention and resolves alive by reflecting on an image of what meditation is like. Envision the transcendent clarity and stillness of deep meditation. You sit balanced, strong, comfortable, and as steady as the rock of Gibraltar, with the breath gently flowing in and out. All cravings and anxieties have evaporated. If you can envision it and believe it, you will achieve it.[28]

If you can't picture yourself in this state, try using an icon of a beloved deity, a Buddha, or great sage. That will provide you with a concrete image to work with.

A positive image reinforced daily can inspire optimism. Optimism, the belief that you can attain a goal, is a great motivator. Over time, the image you have cultivated sinks deeply into the mind. The characteristics that you have associated with the image begin to manifest.

Study

Read sacred texts and books on meditation. Biographies of great yogis, sages, and saints are especially helpful. Rereading key texts – *Yoga Sutras*, *Bhagavad Gita*, or any text that informs and inspires you – is recommended. Take classes, workshops, and retreats with teachers

---

[28] This is a paraphrase of the famous quote by the author, Napoleon Hill, "*Whatever the mind of man can conceive and believe, it can achieve.*"

who are experienced in meditation. When the mind is persuaded of the goal and the effectiveness of meditation, it will want to keep up the practice.

Prayer, Worship, and Ritual

Prayer brings the powerful benefits of bonding – acceptance, dedication, faithfulness, and love – to our relationship with the Self.

Rituals and worship touch us in a way that reason cannot. They breathe life into subtle realities by giving them physical expression as meaningful symbols and actions. Symbolism allows us to understand subtle truths on conscious *and* nonverbal subconscious levels. Prayer, worship, and ritual integrate truths on every level that we exist.

They can be added to your meditation routine or done at another time.

Home Environment

Surroundings influence intention. Take a quick survey of what's in your home. What type of art populates your walls? Your meditation space should reflect the nature and beauty of meditation. Surround yourself with objects that call to mind harmony, peace, and joy.

Think of your meditation space as a sanctuary where you will always find refuge and tranquility.

The Sounds of Meditation

Listen to CDs of mantras, chants, and other uplifting music. Isn't it true that you often go through the day repeating a song you heard on the radio, even if you don't care for it? Why not let that habit of mind that work for you?

Rhythms, melodies, and lyrics reach deep into the mind where it becomes a force that helps shape behavior. If what reaches the subconscious is inspiring, it will fuel the motivation to practice.

THE ESSENTIAL TRIAD
Intention, Attention, and Nonjudgmental Attitude

These three pillars for success in meditation create the optimal inner environment for the meditative state to flourish.

Intention

Intention is directed inspiration. Intention mobilizes physical, psychological, and spiritual energy toward a goal. It is the fuel for regularity and the backdrop for every meditation session.

Intention begins with a vision you'd like to see materialize, an aspiration that inspires hope and optimism. The power of love, enthusiasm, and confidence is unleashed by such a vision.

Intention in meditation serves a purpose similar to a GPS. Not only does a GPS guide you to your destination, it redirects you if you wander off course. If you don't input the destination, the GPS can't help you. In the same way, affirm your objective in meditating at the beginning of every sitting to set your course, and *within* every sitting whenever you stray off course. But, intention remains wishful thinking without resolve.

Resolve is a firm decision, a bridge between intent and action. It can only be made after assessing the factors involved in the option you are considering. Concerning meditation, you need to be unambiguous regarding its benefits *and* what it takes to attain them. Gather the facts concerning the why's and how-to's of meditation, honestly assess your strengths and weaknesses, and come to a conclusion regarding what you're *really* ready to do.

See that your resolves are realistic. Too high, and you're doomed to fail. If they're too low, it means that you have underestimated yourself. You'll lose incentive. Give yourself the compliment of a challenge. You're looking to stretch, but not strain.

Resolves grow stronger with the choices you make daily. *You choose* to begin a practice of meditation. *You choose* to be regular in that practice. *You choose* to keep your attention focused on the object of meditation. It's in your hands. Make the choices that advance you to your goal.

Nurture your resolves through repeated affirmations. Envision yourself succeeding. Look to role models for inspiration. Exercise faith. Look within and summon your inner strength to continue on the path.

When the directed inspiration of intention is coupled with firm resolve, it is called a *sankalpa*.

Attention

Attention follows intention. Attention means to be aware of – to notice, or be present to – any stimulus that draws our awareness outward to sense objects or inward to the contents of the mind. Meditation is sustained attention directed to one thought, object, or image.

It might seem like this would limit or restrict awareness, but it intensifies it. By focusing attention on one point, we become *more* aware. Sustained awareness unlocks the capacity of the mind to examine deeper realities.

In contrast, our awareness is typically limited and clouded by biases, non-sequential notions, emotions, images, and memories that run through the mind. In meditation these limiting factors are gradually transcended. We are treated to the gifts that clear, focused awareness brings.

Nonjudgmental Attitude

This book refers to this mindset in the context of a meditation session as the Golden Moment. Its benefits can't be overemphasized.

Creating an inner environment that is free from judgment goes a long way toward calming and clearing the mind. In a judgmental mindset, we sit as judge and jury, labeling some things as good, others as bad. We do so as if we had a crystal ball that revealed the motives behind everyone's actions and the ultimate outcome of all events. Judgmental attitudes may contain the seeds of arrogance, impatience, and ignorance. On the other hand, a nonjudgmental mindset encourages compassion, empathy, and love. Wisdom, the uncovering of the "whys" in life, depends on this attitude.

The nonjudgmental mindset is also key to overcoming shortcomings. We are born with both strengths and weaknesses. It's evident that strengths exist to overcome weaknesses (and to serve others). The benefits of shortcomings may not be so apparent. Central to spiritual life is the knowledge that weaknesses can help develop virtues. For example, how can we fully understand unconditional love until we find a way to overcome our resistance to forgiving someone who hurt us?

When we meditate, we tend to judge the mind's meanderings as wrong or evil. Once thoughts are labeled as wrong, we struggle to suppress them. We can't overcome negative thoughts by suppressing them. They'll simply wait in a dark corner of the mind and cause problems later on. When they do reappear, they will be stronger.

Instead, learn to be a neutral witness to the mind. Don't judge thoughts that arise in meditation as good or bad. They are just thoughts. Calmly accept them.

The gentle, accepting inner environment of the nonjudgmental mindset allows submerged thoughts to rise to consciousness. Like bubbles in an unopened bottle of soda, many of these thoughts are not visible to our normal awareness. Meditation opens the cap. Enjoy the bubbles. Gradually, the nonjudgmental attitude will become a central aspect of your life and will transform it.

The Essential Triad in the Meditation Routine

These three principles are integrated into the routines presented in this book.

- Opening Chants: affirm intention and focus attention. Devotional chants open the heart, cultivate surrender and humility, and affirm resolves.
- Pranayama: brings energy to the mind and helps make it more tranquil, clear, and focused.
- The Golden Moment #1: establishes the nonjudgmental attitude.
- Silent Meditation: develops attention.
- Golden Moment #2: puts you more closely in touch with the inner witness, solidifies the benefits of meditation, and reinforces the nonjudgmental mindset.
- Closing Peace Chants: helps integrate the meditation experience into daily life, develops compassion, and is a service to others.

Diagnose Meditation Problems Using the Essential Triad

Since unsteady focus can be a symptom of any three factors, you can use your understanding of them to assess and correct problems in meditation.

If you notice that the mind is wandering, but allow it roam anyway, it is because you gave in to the mind's impulse. You lost *intention* and gave in to the mind's *desire*.

If the mind wandered but you don't know how or when it happened, it is primarily due to lack of *attention*. You didn't notice the moment when the mind began to stray.

If you find yourself emotionally engaged and fixated on a thought, if you are lost in an inner debate, or are preoccupied with thoughts of a person or event, you have lost the *nonjudgmental attitude*.

Identify the weakness and apply the appropriate remedy.

Loss of intention. Affirm your goal. Restate it mentally or out loud. Reflect on what you are saying. Don't miss any opportunity to reset your inner GPS and carry on.

Loss of attention. Practice bringing the mind into the present moment. Keep it simple. Resolve that you will do one thing – right now – and do it mindfully. Say your mantra *once* being as fully present to it as you can. Watch *just one* inhalation with full awareness. *Feel* the physical sensation of sitting.

Loss of nonjudgmental attitude. The fact that you became emotionally involved is a sign that an attachment became active. Attachments can be dealt with two ways: analysis, and surrender. You can use either or a combination of both, depending on your temperament.

In analysis, you seek the cause of the disturbance. Ask yourself, "*Why is my mind preoccupied with this – and why now?*" Don't accept the first answer as final. Probe deeper. Keep asking. The real answer is usually hidden behind those of lesser importance.

The other way to neutralize attachments is through surrender. Be present and open to the wisdom of the moment. Look for lessons to be learned. Ask for God's help in overcoming the attachment. Accept that you are given whatever you need for your welfare, even if it is unpleasant. The moment you accept what comes, the mind finds peace.

Every meditator experiences pitfalls. You're learning, growing, and getting stronger every day. Continue with your meditation practice and you will certainly experience the benefits of intention, attention, and the nonjudgmental mindset: clarity of purpose, increased willpower, greater power of concentration, acceptance, lovingkindness, compassion, and surrender. These virtues, all within you, will bloom.

MEDITATION IN ACTION
Karma Yoga:
The Science of Actions and Their Consequences

Karma[29] means both actions and their reactions. Karma *Yoga* is based on a profound understanding of the interplay of motives, actions, and consequences. This is a many-faceted subject that encompasses every aspect of our lives.

Karma Yoga is the path of selfless, dedicated service. It is *selfless* in that motives are not based on a narrow, self-interested view of life's responsibilities, challenges, and opportunities. It is *dedicated* since the fruits of actions are offered to God or humanity.

What does this have to do with meditation? In Yoga, meditation doesn't appear as a practice isolated from daily life. That's because not much progress is made if we take one step forward in meditation and one back after contending with the concerns and difficulties of life.

Karma Yoga obliges us to look at what we do, why we do it, and the ramifications of our actions. It asks us to be skillful in living life.

> *Yoga is perfection in action.*
> Bhagavad Gita, 2.50

Perfection in action is not about being mistake-free.[30] If that were the case, no one could ever hope to live up to the *Gita's* teaching. The notion of perfection that most of us carry is a burden based on a misunderstanding. Life is not a test where we need to score one hundred-percent to be worthwhile human beings. The perfection the *Gita* speaks of is based on three factors: selfless motives, skillful means, and doing good.

A perfect act:
- Begins with a thought: a motive to serve the welfare of others.

---

[29] See, *karma*, in the *Sanskrit Glossary*.

[30] Making a mistake and having a shortcoming are not the same thing, although we often use the word "mistake" when we are really referring to a weakness. If someone is cheating on their spouse and gets caught, he or she might say, "I made a mistake." But it's not that they confused their spouse with the other person. They succumbed to a weakness.

Mistakes are made due to our shortcomings, incomplete information, faulty memory, lapses in logic, or misperception.

Shortcomings are moral and ethical weaknesses rooted in the shortsightedness of attachments.

- Is achieved through skillful means.
- Ends with a positive result: benefit to someone, and at least no harm to anyone.

Motive. A motive can be either selfish or selfless. Most of the time, our motives are a varying mix of selfish and selfless. The problem is that even seemingly benign selfishness can cause us to suffer. There's a corner of the mind that keeps track of what we do and what happens to us in consequence. What we may not have noticed is that this part of us is deeply concerned with fairness. It checks to see if we have been properly recompensed for what we do. Unfortunately, its standard for what constitutes fair is based on a habit of valuing the likes and dislikes of the ego, not what's best for the common welfare. It takes a massive amount of psychic energy to keep this corner of the mind satisfied. Its mental record-keeping is the root of much of the anxiety and bitterness in our lives. It is a fear based attitude that often expresses as, "If I don't look out for myself, who will?" Let's examine what happens when self interest influences the mind, and then contrast it with selflessness.

Selfish motives predispose us to value immediate rewards over long term benefit and self-concern over the welfare of others. We see only what's important to us personally, not necessarily what's best for us, and others. To make matters worse, ego-centered motives result in repeated disappointment and disillusionment because expectations for personal gain are inevitably spoiled by renewed cravings to repeat an achievement, the fear of losing what we've gained, and unwelcome outcomes that we can't control.

Selfless motives are inclusive. The ramifications that actions have on others and the environment is given (*at least*) equal weight as self-interest. The shift from selfish to selfless motives doesn't exclude us. We're an integral part of the common good that we strive to serve. We're just not the center of attention, not the axis around which life in the universe revolves. The truth is better than that, but we won't experience it until we nudge the ego off of its throne. When we do, we discover what the *Tao Te Ching* describes as the empty space that makes the wheel and the cup useful. The empty space in us rightfully belongs to the Self, our True Nature. When we're free of the limited desires of the ego, we're ready to fully accept the wisdom of the Infinite that guides us throughout life.

To prevent the interests of the ego from being the primary guide in our lives, we turn our attention to higher motives. The importance all faith traditions place on self-surrender and on the Golden Rule, prevents ego centered interests from ruling our lives and negatively affecting others.[31]

Selfless acts gradually transform the ego. As the narrow view of selfish interest dissolves, we become integrated human beings who naturally seek greater harmony, prosperity, and happiness for all.[32]

Means. Selfless motives are not enough for an act to be considered "perfect." We need skillful means. There is a story of a man who felt compassion for a caterpillar struggling to break free of its cocoon. Wishing to hasten the creature's exit, he took his pocketknife and very carefully cut a slit in the cocoon. What he didn't know was that a caterpillar can't survive outside its cocoon until it is fully ready to emerge as a butterfly. The caterpillar did not survive his loving attempt at freeing it. His motive was fine, but his skill was lacking.

To develop the ability to properly assess what's needed in situations as well as our capacity to act successfully, spiritual traditions always include practices to develop focus, teachings that reveal human nature, and moral and ethical guidelines. We should also continue to study and practice the skills we need to better fulfill whatever job we hold or service we perform.

Results. With selfless motivation and skillful means, our chances of bringing benefit and no harm greatly increase. We need to be on guard, however. Assessing results requires a keen awareness of the short and long-term consequences of our thoughts, words, and deeds. It is easy to mistake a pleasurable result for a beneficial one.

---

[31] In Yoga, self-surrender is called I*shwara pranidhanam* (sutra 1.23). It teaches to put Ishwara, God, first. In other words, we learn to live by faith, from our center, which is wisdom, rather than from the transient desires of the ego. Surrender to the Higher Will, or to go with the flow of life, are common principles in all faith traditions. Jesus taught it as, *Seek the Kingdom of God and his righteousness first and all these things will be added to you*. Matthew, 6.33.

Forms of the Golden Rule, *Do unto others as you would have them do unto you*," are also found in all faith traditions. To follow this foundational teaching requires self knowledge, empathy, compassion, selflessness, courage, and patience.

[32] The ideal of selfless service includes you. You have a duty to take care of your body and mind to serve. Rest, recreation, and planning for your future security are all part of the thinking of a selfless mind. It's selfish expectations that are dropped. In Karma Yoga, you take care of yourself so that you can serve others. Even meditating is done as a Karma Yoga practice. We better ourselves so that we can better serve others.

The beneficial is one thing; the pleasant is another. These two, differing in their ends, both prompt to action. Blessed are they that choose the beneficial; they that choose the pleasant miss the goal.
Katha Upanishad

By definition (in spiritual teachings, at least), the good that comes from pleasurable experiences is short-term and contributes little to spiritual maturity. Beneficial acts improve someone's material security, physical and psychological well-being, and advance spiritual growth.

The Universal Dimension of Selflessness

As we practice KarmaYoga, our actions and the motives behind them, take on universal proportions. By serving selflessly, we cooperate with Nature's law. All of Nature is based on giving. The cloud gives rain to help the earth nurture its harvests. The sun gives light and warmth for all life. The apple tree after years of effort, freely offers its fruit, not demanding that we eat it. When we give without selfish expectations, we are in harmony with the highest law of nature.

Symptoms of Selfish Motives

How do we know when a selfish thought has motivated us? The seeds of selfishness will eventually manifest as anxiety, fear, greed, lust, envy, anger — any negative emotion. We suffer when the ego wants its own way, but doesn't get it. When the ego's notions of what should be collide with reality, we experience grief. *It is also largely these self-centered notions that generate the distracting thoughts that disturb meditation.* When we practice Karma Yoga, these thoughts are flushed to the surface where they can be analyzed and/or let go of.

One effective way to bring selfish thoughts to light is to ask yourself this question whenever your mind is disturbed: *"What is it that I wanted that I didn't get?"* Don't accept the first answer, not even the second. Keep probing until you find the root cause, the root desire that lead to the mental disturbance.

The Joy in Serving

The greatest lesson of selfless service is the discovery that there is joy *in* serving, not *from* serving. Karma Yoga isn't a reward-for-selfless-act scheme. We serve, love, and give and leave it at that. Rewards will come, but they are not the motivation. Every practitioner of Karma Yoga soon experiences that true giving (giving without expectation), brings joy beyond understanding.

It might seem that a karma yogi is the most selfish person. The goal seems self-centered. We certainly can say that yogis *are* selfish in striving to be selfless. They desire to be desireless. The paradox is that when this desire is fulfilled, selfish desires will have vanished. The yogi, liberated from ignorance, becomes the most qualified person to serve the welfare of others.

Karma Yoga as Test Lab

Another benefit of Karma Yoga is that it tests the depth and quality of spiritual attainments. It's easy to be peaceful when everything is going our way. Selfless service tests the depth of our spiritual maturity by bringing us into contact with obstacles, setbacks, and difficult behavior. The true test of character is how we behave when we are faced with challenge and loss.

There's a story of the yogi with a bad temper.

He lived on the outskirts of a small village. The inhabitants were happy to support his needs, but also a wary of his famous quick temper.

He felt bad to be causing such grief. Believing that he needed to deepen his meditation to overcome his weakness, he left for the nearby mountains. He found a suitable cave and began an intense practice, meditating twelve hours a day.

Five years passed. One day, he descended from the mountain and approached the village. The townspeople were excited to see him and curious to know what he experienced in his solitude.

I've conquered anger, he said confidently in response to the question.

Really, asked a young girl.

Yes.

Sir, you were away so long. In all that time, you didn't lose your temper?

No, child. As I said, I've conquered anger.

Not even once? Maybe a mosquito bit you and you became annoyed.

Why do you keep asking me? I said it already, I've conquered anger!

OK, sir. I understand.

The girl's persistent questioning revealed the weakness in the yogi's strategy to overcome anger. In the cave, there was nothing to test him. Like him, we need to be active in the world to grow.

Every Act Should be Karma Yoga

One common misconception regarding Karma Yoga is that it is about providing a service for free or volunteering for charitable organizations. Karma Yoga is not about working for no pay. We can't serve, let alone get along in this world, without physical resources. We need to eat, have a home, rest, and enjoy some rejuvenating recreation to be fit to serve others. The question is not whether you receive a paycheck, what's crucial is the motive behind the actions. Every act should be Karma Yoga, and it can be, if the motive is for the benefit of others.

That's why you don't have to change your job, or do something "yogic" or "spiritual" to practice Karma Yoga. Do what you normally need to do, but make it a selfless, dedicated act. No other branch of Yoga can transform your entire life into a spiritual practice the way that Karma Yoga can. Karma Yoga alone can take you to Self-realization.

Words to Live By

The objective in practicing Karma Yoga is not to create good karma, although that is where it usually begins. It is to transcend karma altogether, to break free of anything that binds or limits consciousness, love, compassion, joy, and peace. If that sounds good to you, if your sense of adventure prompts you to travel to the farthest borders of Yoga, consider making this teaching a guide for life:

SUCCESS IS IN THE DETAILS

Live for the sake of others. Spend a little time everyday for your own health and peace, and then share it with all.
Sri Swami Satchidananda

DIET:
What's on Your Plate and What's in Your Mind are Related

Success in meditation is enhanced by a diet that encourages the mind to be still and clear. For centuries, yogis have recommended a natural, lacto-vegetarian diet as best for rapid and sure progress. To understand why, we need to discuss three important terms: *sattwa*, *rajas*, and *tamas*. These three, known collectively as the *gunas* (literally, strand or thread), are the fundamental forces or qualities of Nature. Respectively representing balance, activity, and inertia, they are reminiscent of neutrons, electrons, and protons.

All activities, as well as foods, are divided into these categories. Concerning diet, foods of a category will influence the mind in a like way. Sattwic foods will tend to leave the mind in a balanced state, rajasic foods will agitate the mind, and tamasic foods will tend to make the mind dull. It follows that the diet best suited for meditation consists mostly of foods in the sattwic category.

Here's a brief summary of which foods fall into each category.

Sattwa
Raw, steamed, lightly sautéed, or roasted vegetables
Grains, beans, lentils, nuts, soy products (If not overly refined.
 If they are, they can become tamasic.)
Fruits, nuts, dairy (in moderation, if tolerated)
Food that is lightly spiced, not too sour or hot

Rajas
Red meat (except beef)
Poultry
Fish and other seafood
Eggs
Spicy food
Onions, garlic
Caffeine

SUCCESS IS IN THE DETAILS

Tamas
Beef, old, cold, over cooked foods
Deep fried foods
Alcoholic drinks

What is on our plate should consist largely of foods in the sattwic category. At the same time, most of us have a tendency toward tamas: fatigue, sluggishness, etc. Therefore, a little rajasic food can help overcome the tamasic aspect. So, it's fine to have a moderate amount of warming and gently stimulating foods such as onions and garlic, and spice, like ginger, cinnamon, or cayenne, in the diet as needed. When the weather is cold and damp (a tamasic state), adding a little rajasic food helps keep the body and mind in balance. The same is true if you are suffering from a cold, also a tamasic state. Adding some spice to your diet will help speed the cold away.

Along with increasing sattwa, a vegetarian diet is best for meditation because it is the most nonviolent. No doubt, life in some form is always taken for us to live. A potato sacrifices its existence for us. It has consciousness, but it's not as evolved as animals or humans. It's something like deep sleep or being under anesthesia.

On the other hand, an animal can sense its impending death. The fear, emotional turmoil, and suffering it undergoes are transferred to its flesh. The anxiety stays in the meat as the vibration of fear, and as bile and other toxic chemicals released during stress. When we eat meat, we absorb all this. That's why eating meat tends to increase aggressiveness and restlessness.

Some people, aware of the suffering the animals undergo, offer a prayer of thanksgiving to the animal for giving its life. Their intention is to make reparation for the animal's suffering with their loving thoughts. They may also believe that their prayers cancel out the karma that eating meat entails. It's true that sincere prayers for these animals can benefit their departed souls, but they cannot completely absolve us from the karma we are bound to face for being a cause of their suffering – especially if the prayers are repeated with the *intent* of being absolved from negative karma.[33] This is truer today than ever before. Most animals raised for food lead lives of great pain and suffering. They lack exercise, are not allowed to interact with other

---
[33] If the intent is personal absolution, you're praying for yourself more than for the animals.

animals, are fed an unnatural diet, given antidepressants and caffeine, and are injected with hormones to artificially accelerate growth and antibiotics to stem disease. If you eat flesh foods, you ingest those chemicals as well.

That said, eating meat does not make you an immoral person unfit for spiritual life. As Jesus said, "*It is not what goes into the mouth that defiles a person, but what comes out of the mouth; this defiles a person.*" (Matthew 15.12). You can succeed in meditation regardless of diet, but food that comes with suffering makes it more difficult. More effort will have to be exerted to overcome the influence of flesh foods.

On the physiological side, meat is an acidic food. Excess acid leads to many diseases and disorders. It irritates the nervous system and can be a causative factor in inflammatory diseases like arthritis and heart disease.

A balanced vegetarian diet provides all the nutrients needed for good health. Fresh, vegetarian foods are brimming with *prana*. The fact that grains can be sprouted and grown, and that seeds have the power to reproduce vegetables is a proof that the life force in vegetarian food is potent. It is prana, more than nutrients, that the body and mind requires. Nutrients are physical manifestations of the more subtle and powerful prana. Meat is a dead food. You can't plant any part of a chicken to get more chicken.

Meat-eating is also an inefficient use of the planet's resources. For example, it takes a tremendous amount of grain and soy to feed the animals destined for our tables. Estimates are that if Americans reduced their intake of meat by ten percent, one-hundred million people could be adequately fed.

Some people advocate vegetarianism based on certain physiologic structures in the human body, contending that they more closely resemble that of herbivores. They compare such anatomical features as relative intestinal length, eyes that are equipped to see in low light, shape of teeth, and the rough-textured tongues of carnivorous animals with herbivores. Although some don't agree, these comparisons present a strong argument that human beings are better suited for assimilating nutrients from non-meat sources. Regardless of these structural considerations, there are many good reasons for eating a balanced vegetarian diet: it leaves the mind clear and calm, causes the least suffering, provides necessary nutrients while being easier to digest, is naturally high in fiber, builds immunity, and is heart healthy.

Sri Swami Sivananda taught that in matters of diet, evolution is better than revolution. It's worth considering a gradual reduction of the amount of meat in your diet. Experiment with the vast number of vegetarian options open to you and note how the change in your diet affects your physical and mental wellbeing.

Your State of Mind When Eating

You will digest your food much better if you eat in a calm state. One reason for saying a meal prayer before eating is that it helps you center yourself. You digest and assimilate better if you are relaxed. A meal prayer accomplishes this and also develops gratitude for the miracle of the earth coming to your table as food. If you don't know a meal prayer, just sit for a minute or two, watch your breath, holding the thought of gratitude to the Mother Earth. Eat mindfully, and chew the food well. My master, Gurudev Satchidananda always said, "It's better to fast than to eat fast."[34]

Avoid the Cranky Cook

The mindset of the cook affects the food. Bad-tempered cooks infect even the most nutritious food with their toxic attitude. Your mind can be affected by these negative thoughts. One good reason to bless the food before eating is that it raises its vibration.

If you're cooking, and get into a testy mood, put food preparation on pause until the feeling passes.

If crankiness and bad attitudes can infect food, a peaceful mind and good attitude can enrich it. Play uplifting music or chant while you cook. Serve the food as a loving offering. Cook the food with love, serve it with love, and eat it with love.

---

[34] You can find an audio of a wonderful meal prayer at www.yogalifesociety.com. Look under the *Sounds of Yoga* tab.

MEDITATION JOURNAL
A Way to Track Your Progress

We're not very good at keeping our resolves. We get distracted. Old habits sneak back in, we become discouraged, and we forget our original intent. The result is that too many of our goals remained unrealized.

If you're intent on making the best of meditation, it's important to make sure that you stay on track every day. It's too easy for one missed meditation to snowball into a month of lost opportunities. A meditation journal is an effective tool to track your progress and speed you to your goals.

Keeping a journal allows you to see how often you slip from your resolves. You might be surprised by how often you miss – or don't miss – fulfilling your intentions. You will be able to quickly catch lapses, analyze how you became sidetracked, and then take the necessary actions to get back on course.

How to Create a Journal
- Start by asking yourself a few questions such as: What is it that I wish to achieve? How many times a day do I intend to meditate and for how long? Are there any changes in diet I wish to make? Would I like to incorporate a daily practice of Hatha Yoga? Attend meditation classes? Study sacred texts?
- You can include traits you'd like to develop and ones you'd like to eliminate. For example, if you tend to be impatient, add cultivating patience to your chart. If you would like to develop greater generosity, that can be added as well.
- Create a chart of your resolves. Then check off each item as you complete it.
- Leave blank space for your reflections.
- You can devise a "corrective action" for lapses, such as adding more time with one of your resolves. For example, increase time for study or pranayama, or add a meditation.

Review your journal at the end of every month and adjust according to your progress and needs.

Lapses are not a sign that you are unsuited for spiritual practice. You can often learn more from failures than from successes. That's why they are valued in Yoga. Lapses are occasions when we can directly encounter, and remedy shortcomings. With the right attitude, there are no failures, just learning experiences.

HATHA YOGA AND MEDITATION

Hatha Yoga is the physical branch of Yoga. It includes bending and stretching postures (*asanas*), breathing exercises (*pranayama*), cleansing practices (*kriyas*), deep relaxation (*yoga nidra*), and techniques to focus and guide prana (*bandhas and mudras*). Hatha Yoga makes the body supple, strong, and relaxed while ridding it of toxins that disturb health and ease. There are many different styles of Hatha Yoga. Some schools don't use the word Hatha.[35] Others consider what they teach a yogic practice, but not Hatha. Regardless of these variations, in this book the term "Hatha" refers to any form of physical practice that:

- Promotes the harmony and integration of body, mind, and Spirit
- Develops focus and clarity of mind
- Teaches techniques for profound relaxation
- Enhances physical health and strength

In Hatha's earlier days, kriyas were emphasized over asanas. The body can't make full use of the benefits of the asanas or pranayama, when there is an excess of toxins. Toxins cause inflammation, stiffness, pain, lethargy, and a cloudy state of mind. Cleansed of toxins, we experience abundant balanced energy and clarity.

Pranayama is one of the treasures of Hatha Yoga. The breathing practices benefit all bodily systems. Especially when practiced with the bandhas and mudras, they are similar in effect to acupuncture. Pranayama also makes the mind alert and clear by promoting the strong, rhythmic flow of prana, which encourages a clear, orderly flow of thoughts.

The higher goal of Hatha Yoga is to purify the subtle nerve currents, the *nadis*. The nadis are similar to the meridians in acupuncture, serving as a communication network, linking the functions of all bodily systems, organs, and tissues. When the function of the nadis is hampered by toxins, the prana can't flow freely. Areas of excess (due to blockages) and depletion of prana are formed resulting in a decline in health and wellbeing. Purified nadis allow both the body and mind to function at optimal levels. These benefits mean that Hatha Yoga is a natural and powerful ally to meditation.

---

[35] The word *hatha* literally means "by force" and does not refer to a particular school of thought. Use of the word suggests performing a physical practice (applying force or effort) to begin to control the mind, as opposed to meditation, which works directly with the mind.

SUCCESS IS IN THE DETAILS

For morning sadhana, it is best to meditate before sunrise and follow that with Hatha Yoga. If you arise after sunrise, or if doing Hatha Yoga is a significant aid to calming your mind, do the Hatha first and then meditate. Still, the benefits of meditating first thing in the day make it a worthwhile goal. First thoughts have a great influence on our state of mind throughout the day.

MINDFUL LIVING
Awaken to Life

Live the present moment wisely and earnestly
The Buddha

Mindfulness is the practice of bringing heightened awareness and clear attentiveness to daily life.[36] Mindfulness brings the skills and benefits gained from meditation, to everyday activities and refines them further. In essence, our lives – what we are doing and thinking, and our reactions to events – become the object of attention.

It might be surprising – or unsettling – to realize that most of the time, we are not present to our own lives. Our experience of life and self is filtered through memories, biases, and random or half-formed thoughts and feelings.

Most of us had our first experience of a banana when we were a baby. Our first taste was a revelation. At that moment, we didn't think of a banana as a fruit, or sweet, or yellow. We simply enjoyed the direct experience of its nature. The second time we had one, our experience had an overlay of memory. We recalled its taste as we ate it, and maybe the sweet smiling face of our mother as she watched us savor it. The full experience of the banana became mixed with thoughts and impressions. The experience of the banana was mixed with our conception of bananas.

This mind-activity is called *vritti* in Yoga.[37] It is the primary mode of mental functioning. Our mind seeks to find ways to label events, people, and feelings for easy reference. It's a very practical function. Life is simpler and saner if we don't have to rethink or reanalyze everything

---

[36] Heightened awareness refers to the scope of consciousness; how much is included in our field of attention. Clear attentiveness refers to the degree of focus of attention.

[37] Vritti (see *Yoga Sutras*, 1.2.), literally means to twirl. It's a colorful, but accurate description of the mental process the mind uses to make sense of life and to understand what brings pleasure or pain. To gain understanding, when the mind encounters a new bit of information, it launches into a twirling dance, looking within for thoughts and experiences that relate to the incoming data. The more relevant bits of data it finds, the deeper its understanding. The product of this activity (also called a vritti) is a concept that is composed of a mixture of true, semi-true, and false data.

While vritti activity is how we usually try to understand life, the yogi, whose mind experiences subtler states of awareness, also has access to insight (*prajna*), direct perceptions that are not mediated by dualistic thinking or biases.

SUCCESS IS IN THE DETAILS

we do. It's not necessary to re-recognize our partner every evening. Their name, appearance, and our memories and feelings about them instantly come up the moment we see them. Our conception of them "arrives" with them.

If we're not vigilant, vritti activity can also lull us to "sleep." Pure inner awareness risks becoming increasingly veiled every time we rely on habit instead of attentiveness, awakened reason, and insight to guide our way. The truth of what the universe is and who we are is colored by past impressions of fear, wishful thinking, half-truths, falsehoods, and misperceptions. We can see examples of this at work in people who hold strong prejudices. They feel safer, superior, inferior, or correct if they regard a person through the lens of gender, race, or nationality (through a biased vritti) rather than as an individual with unique qualities. Mindfulness is a powerful remedy for this kind of thinking.

Mindfulness is the practice of being fully present to life. Cultivate the habit of paying better attention to whatever it is that you are doing: driving, listening to a friend, or laying carpet, for example. Mindfulness also includes a heightened awareness of your reactions to people and the events that capture your attention. Why did you react negatively to the new person at work, with longing to the song of the robin outside your window, or nostalgically to the photo of your high school graduation?

Mindfulness:

Supports Meditation

If we meditate one hour a day and then let the mind run amok for the remaining twenty-three, we'll have a difficult time attaining and maintaining a clear, still mind in meditation.

Resist the temptation to be on autopilot with everything you do. Cutting uniform slices of carrot for the soup develops attention just as repeating your mantra does. Attentive carrot slicing helps your meditation, while meditation helps you become a better cook. Extend this mindful awareness to all aspects of your day. See what wonderful things happen.

Banishes Boredom

There is an adage, *"Attention develops interest."* Through mindfulness, activities that we regard as boring, a waste of time, or distasteful can be redeemed. Instead of being annoying, they become vehicles for cultivating positive states of mind.

How does mindfulness lead to this miracle? It engages the mind's capacity to probe the object of its focus which illumines otherwise missed dimensions of a situation that fascinates and informs. It's much like reading a textbook, or watching a documentary that doesn't seem interesting at first. As we learn more, our interest perks up. We become absorbed in the subject and find that in the end, we learned a lot and enjoyed ourselves.

From mindfulness we learn the extent to which emotional states like boredom are, in reality, under our control.

Cultivates Compassion and Self-awareness

The practice of mindfulness naturally extends to our motives, and to the impact of our thoughts, words, and actions. We will begin to notice how selfish thoughts – often rooted in craving or pain – cause pain to others and us. Our own struggles to grow deepen compassion. Empathy effortlessly flows from our hearts. We care for the well-being of others. We experience the entire creation as our family.

Makes Us More Efficient

The yogi's mind always looks to get more done with less effort. Look for more efficient ways to make your famous minestrone soup, paint your living room, mow the lawn, or write that report for work. Can you combine trips to the cleaner with other chores? What is the best, most efficient route to get your errands done? Have some fun with this. You'll save time and energy, avoid a great deal of stress, and get more done.

Gives the Gift of the Golden Present

Mindfulness roots us in the present. The past is gone and the future hasn't arrived. This moment is all we have, it's where we live, and where the wisdom of life continually seeks to guide our way. In normal waking consciousness, this present moment is as close as we come to the eternal, timeless state, our True Self. That's why, if we can be fully present to the moment, fear, anxiety, and stress dissolve.

QUALITIES OF SUCCESSFUL MEDITATORS

It may seem that some people are natural born meditators. Are there qualities that are best suited for meditation? Yes, but rarely do they appear full-blown from birth. They are already in you, but they need to be nurtured to realize full expression.

There are six characteristics to explore: fervor, humility, generosity, fidelity, creativity, and patience. We've touched on a few of them already. They are found in successful women and men in all fields of endeavor. These are qualities that are admired in role models. Let them serve as an invitation to become the hero of your own life.

Fervor

Fervor is a persistent longing to reach a goal. This powerful motivator is born from a state of unrest. Until our goal is realized, we don't feel *fully* at home, at rest, or whole. The longing we experience when we are separated from our beloved is a form of fervor. Repeatedly, our thoughts are drawn to our loved one. We might find temporary relief in work or other distractions, but if the separation continues for an extended period, our consciousness becomes dominated by the feeling that something vital is missing. The mind and heart, now one-pointed in their intention, spur us to take whatever action we can to reunite with the one we love.

We can cultivate fervor for meditation by contemplating this formula:

Life, sooner or later, brings suffering.
+
Meditation offers a way to transcend suffering.

Only Self-realization can permanently douse the flames of suffering. The love of family and friends, and success in our career may come close, but life's changes still disrupt our comfort and security with unwelcome twists and turns. Even if they didn't, we can't seem to quench the endless cavalcade of desires that we hope will bring our minds peace.

Something is still missing. We are not fulfilled – filled full. After suffering many disappointments, we begin to see that a life built solely on satisfying desires only brings temporary victories. When we accept this, we experience an interest and then a fervor to find something deeper that can satisfy the longing for peace.

This may appear to be a life-denying philosophy that regards the world as evil. On the contrary, it's a matter of seeking the maximum happiness, but not from a lifetime accumulation of temporary pleasures. Unshakable happiness, the happiness beyond understanding, is rooted in experiencing our essential oneness with the source of life. Only when we are firmly rooted in the experience of the Self, can we truly enjoy the pleasures of life. Pleasure comes, and we are at peace; pleasure goes, and we are at peace. That is freedom.

As we allow this truth to inform our expectations and attitudes, fervor develops and we are inspired to meditate to end suffering.

Fervor doesn't mean becoming a recluse or an obsessive fanatic. One of the beautiful things about being a meditator is that most people won't even know that you practice. Quietly go about your daily life, sitting twice a day. The special serenity that you radiate may be the only thing that gives you away.

Humility

One of the main stumbling blocks to finding success in meditation is that we can't fully accept the power that lies in its simplicity. We are conditioned to believe that solutions to problems will come from science, technology, and from experts who have mastered principles beyond our understanding. How can sitting with our attention focused on the breath, an image, or sound transform our lives? Shouldn't dissolving suffering be more complex? The challenge is to be humble enough to accept the simplicity of meditation.

Humility doesn't crave acknowledgement, but knowledge. In this, it is intimately connected to the tantalizing capacity to be wonderstruck. It is a state of mind that revels in learning, in being surprised by the enormity, power, mystery, creativity, and beauty of life. It regards the unknown, not with terror, but with keen interest and anticipation. We know what being struck with wonder is like: Words fall away. The mind becomes still and alert. The breath stops (hence the word, *breathtaking*).

We are left with wonder (*not* with wondering). The mind cannot grasp the experience in its entirety, but it doesn't matter. We surrender to the experience. That's part of its joy. Wonder is a taste of the transcendent. A mind that can be struck with wonder is a mind that can experience the highest peaks of meditation.

Generosity

Generosity means to willingly put aside limited personal desires to create a greater, more fulfilling reality. Generosity knows that nothing is lost by selfless giving. There is only gain. Generosity is a companion of compassion. We give when we empathize. We are born with an instinctive impulse to alleviate suffering, but that inclination is often blocked by suspicion, fear, and personal cravings.

Generosity is more than donating to worthwhile causes. When we devote our time and energy to listen to the problems of others, allow someone with only one item to move ahead of us at the market, or rejoice in the happiness of others, we are exercising generosity.

Meditation requires a generous spirit. We put aside what the mind wants, to pay attention to the object of meditation. Practicing generosity in life will lead to better meditation. Conversely, meditation will naturally lead to greater generosity.

Fidelity

Fidelity is continued loyalty to a person, cause, or belief. It expresses as steadiness, integrity, strength, dependability, sticking to a goal, and keeping your word. People who have developed fidelity have the perseverance and the courage to stay with a task to its completion.

Meditation can transform your mind and with it, your life. To experience these changes, we need to eliminate the ingrained habits that obstruct transformation. Without fidelity we can never replace habitual, knee-jerk thinking with a mind that is bright, clear, and incisive. To understand the role fidelity plays in creating this change, we need to discuss how habits are formed.

Think of the mind as a lump of clay. As a thought moves across the mind, it is like a pin scratching a path across its surface. Repeated thoughts cut through the same path creating deep grooves. Habits are difficult to change because mental energy tends to fall into, and flow along, the deepest grooves, dragging our attention with it. In new meditators, meditation grooves are not very deep. With regular practice, these grooves become deeper. Meanwhile, like unused jungle trails that become overgrown with plant life, old unwanted grooves begin to fill in. Old habits, with their strength now diminished, fade while new ones become strong. Over time, the new habits become so deeply ingrained that they become part of our character. The highest benefits of meditation cannot be realized without meditation becoming a deeply ingrained habit.

Following are a few suggestions to cultivate fidelity.

- Follow through. Finish the book you've started, go to the dinner party you dread, complete the course on knitting even though the teacher bores you. This practice builds character and strength of mind.
- When you give your word, keep it. It's not always easy. Think twice before speaking.
- Digging shallow wells won't give you water. Don't scatter your energy by flirting with commitments. Frequently changing goals doesn't offer much fruit. You won't make the best and quickest progress in meditation by taking a little here and there from different schools of thought. That can lead to confusion as well as dissipation of energy. Superficially, meditation traditions *are* different, but in essence, they are one. You might miss their depth by dabbling. Go deep and *experience* the core. Another benefit of sticking to one thing is that you develop the capacity to prevent obstacles in meditation. The mind becomes so steady, clear, and one-pointed that you don't have to exert much energy to overcome challenges. Like water off a duck's back, they naturally roll off such a mind.
- Analyze desires for change. Carefully and patiently ask yourself why you want to look for another job, relationship, or Yoga school. Sometimes, there are good reasons, especially if it means protecting yourself from harm. Much of the time, however, it is the mind being restless or resisting change, even positive change.
- Don't become obsessed with quick results. Nothing great was ever accomplished overnight. Tend to the process; the results will take care of themselves.
- Make use of group support. Associate with others who share your goal.

SUCCESS IS IN THE DETAILS

- Don't set yourself up for failure. Be honest with yourself. Take up goals that you truly believe in. Don't do things just because they are popular, or your friends encourage you to do them. If you do, you'll lack the steadfast zeal needed to succeed. Even with meditation, if it's not for you at this time, why punish yourself with it? Maybe you will be drawn to it later.
- Cultivate a consistent practice. While it's fine to experience other techniques from time to time to expand your understanding of meditation, your daily routine should be stable. Not rigid, stable. The length and content of your routine will evolve over time as you learn and experience more. What doesn't work well is to make frequent and/or haphazard changes. Success belongs to those whose focus doesn't become scattered.
- Make sure that the head and the heart agree. Your heart should experience an attraction, exhilaration, and palpable sense of optimism with your path. At the same time, the mind should approve.
- Have faith in your path. It helps if your path has an established history. The practice of meditation involves many subtleties. A tradition that has proven itself over time is invaluable. You will enjoy the benefits of having a well tread, clearly marked path. This will also provide a context that helps integrate the changes that meditation brings.[38]

Cultivating fidelity brings challenges. The mind will present all sorts of reasons to skip a meditation or give up meditating altogether. Be prepared; *you will* experience doubts, lapses, and restlessness. If you act only according to how you *feel*, you'll miss many sittings and benefits. Keep in mind that because something is difficult, doesn't mean that it's wrong for you. The mind resists going outside its comfort zone. If you've investigated the pros and cons of your decision well, stick to it.

---

[38] This does not imply that every valid path is simply a carbon copy of past tradition. Tradition is a source of tried-and-true knowledge and inspiration, but teachings are not meant to be enshrined in a spiritual museum. Our allegiance should be to the spirit of the law, not its letter. It is healthy for a lineage to repackage its teachings to address its time and culture. It helps keep them alive and relevant. Though the way teachings are expressed may change, the essence remains the same.

Creativity

Creativity is not just for artists. It is a foundation of problem solving. Don't we need creativity to deal with our children when they get into mischief? It is also useful when we try to live within our means when inflation outruns our income, when we have an unexpected pregnancy, or lose our job.

Creativity requires freedom. The mind needs to be free to envision what might be without getting lost in misperception or pure fantasy. Creativity harnesses the powers of imagination and hope to manifest a reality that is best suited to our time, place, and circumstance.

Creativity also requires courage. The fear of failure smothers creative impulses. Let the mind soar. Let it conjure realities that *could* exist. Why not envision yourself as a successful meditator?

Building and maintaining a meditation practice exercises creativity. When you strive to be regular in practice, challenges emerge: *How do I take care of my partner, the dogs, pay the bills, and at the same time tend to my meditation practice? What can I do to make it possible for me to be regular in my meditation practice?*

Successful meditators can be as creative as a Picasso, or Mozart. They have faced every excuse the mind can conjure to keep the body in bed in the morning. They have encountered disappointment, setbacks, and doubt, and found ways to persevere. Through it all, they have managed to find joy and freedom in regular practice. If that's not creativity, what is?

Find inspiration from master musicians, athletes, dancers, cooks, or entrepreneurs. Take in beautiful music, painting, sculpture, prose, and poetry to open the nonverbal, creative aspects of the mind.

Patience

Patience is not just an exercise in waiting. It is not about doing nothing until something happens. Patience is preparation, the marshaling of inner resources. It is alert receptive awareness poised to respond.

Every meditation session brings benefit. Those benefits, like seeds that do much of their essential work underground, remain unseen until later. Fixating daily on results can become an obstacle. Know where you are headed, but focus on the process, not the goal. You will reach your objective more quickly. Learn to value and appreciate each step of the journey. Soon you will find that the fruits of meditation are not only different – *they are greater* – than you imagined.

SAMADHI
MEDITATION'S FINISH LINE

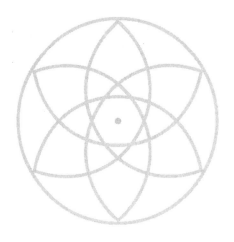

ABSORPTION, INSIGHT, WISDOM

*A lump of salt thrown into water dissolves and the lump
cannot be taken out, but wherever we taste the water it is salty.
In the same way, O Maitreyi, the individual self, dissolved,
is the Eternal – pure consciousness, infinite, and transcendent.*
Brihadaranyaka Upanishad

The above quote is one way of describing samadhi, the technical term for enlightenment. Samadhi means to be absorbed. It is the merging of subject and object; of individual consciousness with the object of attention.

When you see the term alone, without any qualifiers, it generally refers to the highest enlightenment (technically, *nirbija* samadhi). The word "samadhi" is also applied to the various less advanced superconscious states. The lower samadhis are a vital way of learning that transcends the intellect without contradicting reason. They are highly refined spiritual "tools" that unveil subtle aspects of reality that resist being minimized or relativized so that they can be grasped by reason. Knowledge resulting from samadhi is referred to as *prajna*, intuitive insight, wisdom, or revelation.

Samadhi is not separate from meditation, but its culmination. The same meditation we have been practicing all along; that brought us a peaceful and clear mind, begins to explore its object of attention, searching for the cause behind the effect. This process is automatic and natural to a one-pointed mind.

It begins with concentration (*dharana*), the practice of learning to fix the mind on one point. The object of attention is something that can be perceived by the senses, or that can be visualized by the mind. In other words, the object of meditation has a form and a name.

When in that same meditation, the mind learns to prolong its attention for a while, we enter the state of meditation proper (*dhyana*). At this stage, our attention has attained a steady, effortless flow. We experience the object as it is, without the mind's propensity for conceptualization (vritti activity).

When our attention becomes absorbed in the object of meditation, we begin the practice of samadhi. The mind penetrates the gross form of the object and it begins to reveal its inner nature, the forces

SAMADHI: MEDITATION'S FINISH LINE

(subtle elements[39]) that brought it into being. Knowledge and wisdom increase.[40] As samadhi deepens, we leave behind the subtle elements. It is at this point that the object of meditation slips away. There are no more insights to be gained from it. Awareness turns to itself. The mind, still and clear, is just aware of awareness. This is a profoundly deep, peaceful, and joyful experience.

Diving deeper within, we come to experience the ego, the sense of individuality. No other thoughts or impressions are in the mind. Words are insufficient to the experience, but we can say that we are simply aware of "I." It is here that we begin to delve into the identity of the perceiver. Who is it that has been meditating and is aware of all these things all these days? Only subconscious impressions remain. We are now at the doorstep of Self-realization. When this samadhi is held long enough, the meditation deepens, the ego vanishes, subconscious impressions dissolve, and we merge in union (yoga) with the Self.

---

[39] In Sanskrit, subtle elements are known as *tanmatras*.

[40] Although the words *knowledge* and *wisdom* are often used interchangeably, we can make a distinction. Knowledge is composed of pieces of information, subtle or gross. Wisdom is concerned with understanding the "whys" of the existence of something. Wisdom guides the use of knowledge so that it brings meaning and benefit.

SAMADHI IN THE YOGA SUTRAS OF PATANJALI

There are one hundred ninety-six sutras in Patanjali's classic text. Since thirty-four discuss various aspects of samadhi, it suggests that this topic is worthy of special attention.

The four categories of samadhi represent a roadmap of key experiences on the journey to Self-realization. When we know the route, we understand what constitutes progress and can make course corrections quickly and accurately.

Details for each of the four categories follow this listing. The word *absorption* is used to translate samadhi. From gross to subtle, they are:

Samprajnata Samadhi. Absorption with thought activity. This is the only category that has subdivisions – it has four. Awareness probes gross and subtle objects, then the mind itself, and finally the ego sense.

Asamprajnata Samadhi. Absorption without thought activity. Conscious activity ceases, only subconscious impressions remain.

Dharmamegha Samadhi. Absorption that confers virtue.

Nirbija Samadhi. Absorption in which the mind and ego sense are transcended. Self-realization is attained.

Category One: Samprajnata Samadhi, Samadhi with Thought

This samadhi is samprajnata, "with thought," because the mind is focused on an object (gross or subtle) — something that can be perceived.

The levels of samprajnata samadhi represent the four essential categories of the material universe.

- **Savitarka**: absorption on gross elements perceivable by the senses.
- **Savichara**: absorption on subtle elements.
- **Sananda**: absorption on the individual mind.
- **Sasmita**: absorption on the ego-sense.

Practitioners begin with the gross objects and, as their meditation deepens, experience the subtler levels.[41]

The insight gained from these samadhis has a clarity, depth, breadth, and immediacy that is nothing like what we acquire from

---

[41] The samprajnata samadhis can be found in sutra 1.17.

ordinary thought processes. We gain knowledge of the nature of the object of contemplation that is direct and complete.

Let's take an example that demonstrates how the mind moves through the four samprajnata samadhis. Let's suppose that the object of meditation is a red rose.

Savitarka, samadhi with examination. In savitarka samadhi, the senses' perception of the flower is left behind for the inner impression—the image of a red rose on the mind. The mind's absorption on the rose initiates a process of deep examination.

In savitarka samadhi, the three facets involved in the perception of gross objects—name, form, and ideas regarding the object—persist. Also remaining, as with all the samprajnata samadhis, is the awareness of meditator, object of meditation, and act of meditating.

Savichara, samadhi with insight. The word *"vichara"* implies progressive movement. From examination of the gross aspects of an object, the mind penetrates the object to examine factors that brought the object into being and that are its essence. This can include the subtle elements and such factors as time and space. In our example, as the meditation progresses, the mind contemplates a subtle essence of the rose—perhaps its redness.

Savichara samadhi provides direct insight into the principles of the evolution of matter.

Sananda, samadhi with bliss. As the mind becomes even more one-pointed and clear, the idea of redness evaporates and, in a natural progression, the mind probes the phenomenon of perception itself. The focus is on the pure (*sattwic*) aspect of the mind. The nature of the pure mind is luminous, tranquil, and joyful; therefore the practitioner experiences joy (*ananda*).

Sasmita, samadhi with ego sense. Finally, as the meditation matures, the next object of examination is the ego-sense (*asmita*), the basis of individual perception. Sasmita samadhi leads to the next category of samadhi: *asamprajnata*.

Category Two: Asamprajnata Samadhi: Samadhi without Thought

In asamprajnata samadhi there are no gross or subtle objects, and no conscious thoughts. Even the ego-sense, the thought of "I," has dissolved. Only subconscious impressions remain.

This state is very close to Self-realization. However, the presence of active subconscious impressions means that the subtle ego structure[42] still exists. There is a chance that the practitioner can fall under the influence of ignorance if these "seeds" are activated by external or internal stimuli.

Category Three: Dharmamegha Samadhi, Cloud of Virtue Samadhi

This samadhi is said to rain down virtue on the practitioner since it brings behavior based on selfishness to an end. In this state, we experience that all facets of creation are immaterial to pure consciousness. They do not and cannot affect or limit consciousness in any way.

Furthermore, we experience a shift in identity from one based on the activities and structures of the mind to the pure, unchanging awareness that is the Self. At this point, we feel the pull of the Absolute, calling us to the experience of union.

Category Four: Nirbija Samadhi, Seedless Samadhi

To attain Self-realization, the subconscious impressions need to be transcended, as well as the impressions created by the lower samadhis. We need to rise above and beyond every thought, conception, memory, and insight regarding who we are to experience oneness with the Absolute.

The definition of this samadhi is found in sutra 1.51, *"With the stilling of even this impression, every impression is wiped out and there is nirbija samadhi."*

---

[42] Referring to *vasanas*. They are a subset of *samskaras*, (subconscious impressions) that are linked together to form habit patterns or personality traits. They are regarded as the immediate cause of rebirth.

THE FOUR STATES OF AWARENESS

There are other ways of describing the experience of deeper states of consciousness. Instead of samadhi, we will use another term to designate the highest consciousness, *turiya*, the fourth. We routinely experience three states of awareness: waking, dreaming, and dreamless sleep. Turiya, pure unbounded consciousness, transcends, and is the backdrop for them all.

When you are awake, the ego identifies with that state, its contents, and the characteristics of the waking world. You go to work, have lunch, talk to friends, make decisions, watch the daily news, and react to what you hear. You feel happy, tired, sad, sick, or wonderful.

When the mind tires, it falls into deep sleep. The waking world *seems* to disappear. You are unaware of the physical surroundings and the conscious mind shuts off. Yet, the ego is still operating, personal identity still exists, but there is not much to identify with. The mind holds only one thought: the thought of nothingness.[43]

When you dream, you enter the third of the four states. In a dream, you can be a rock star, a celebrated chef, stalked by a tiger, or win an Academy Award. The "real" world and the deep sleep world have vanished and are replaced by another, very different one. The ego identifies with the activities and environment of the dream.

Turiya is experienced when the other three states are transcended. Once turiya is realized in its fullness, you never cease to experience your True Nature as Cosmic Consciousness. The other three states will still be in business, but you don't lose the experience of the Self as your self.

---

[43] Refers to sutra 1.10, *That mental modification which depends on the thought of nothingness is sleep.*

THE ROOTS OF
YOGA MEDITATION

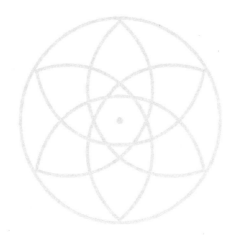

TRADITIONAL TEXTS THAT SPEAK ON MEDITATION

The two most influential Yoga texts that speak on meditation theory and practice are the *Yoga Sutras of Patanjali* and the *Bhagavad Gita*. They are well known and respected worldwide and have been used by seekers for centuries.

We will also take a brief look at the *Hatha Yoga Pradeepika* and the *Upanishads*. The first has gained in importance in the West in recent years due to its emphasis on Hatha Yoga. In India, the *Upanishads* are revered as containing the highest spiritual knowledge.

YOGA SUTRAS OF PATANJALI

The *Yoga Sutras* presents the essential teachings on the nature of the mind, the universe, and of suffering and the way to transcend it. It is divided into four sections, or *padas*: Absorption, Practice, Accomplishments, and Independence. Compiled by the sage, Patanjali, it presents teachings that have been a common thread of virtually every school of Yoga for the past 2000 years. Often called Raja Yoga, the Royal Yoga, it describes a holistic approach to spirituality. Following is a selection of sutras that pertain to meditation with brief commentary. Interested readers should seek out at least one or two translations with full commentaries for further study.

The stilling[44] of the modifications of the mind-stuff is Yoga. Then the Seer (Self) abides in its own nature. At other times, the Self appears to assume the forms of the mental modifications. 1.2 - 1.4.

This is the heart and soul of Yoga. These sutras give both the goal and means to attain it. When the mind is still, clear, and peaceful, we realize who we are. We experience union (*yoga*) with our True Nature. At other times, we identify with whatever thoughts and images occupy the mind at the moment.

We tend to think of the mind as a bio-computer, hardware into which data is downloaded, analyzed, and filed for future reference. This is true enough, but Raja Yoga adds another dimension. The mind is also like a mirror, reflecting both the outside world and thoughts, bringing them to the light of consciousness. The mind also has the capacity to reflect our True Nature. When the mind is tranquil and focused, we experience the Self that has always been in us, *as* us.

These mental modifications are stilled by practice and nonattachment. 1.12.

Mental modifications (*vritti*) are the activities or fluctuations of individual consciousness.[45] The *Sutras* offer this two-pronged approach to attaining the stillness necessary for Self-realization.

---

[44] See *nirodha* in the *Sanskrit Glossary* and the chapter on *Redefining Stillness*.

[45] For more on *vritti*, see the *Sanskrit Glossary*.

Of these two, effort toward steadiness is practice. 1.13.

Steadiness in practice refers to focusing the mind in meditation, the cultivation of regularity, and to developing an unwavering nonjudgmental awareness of the mind's activities, especially the ego's harmful effect on our peace of mind.

By using the word "effort," this sutra suggests that success in Yoga does not come by accident or through wishful thinking. Nothing great was ever achieved without an expenditure of time and energy.

It is significant that this sutra doesn't refer to any sectarian traditions. Patanjali doesn't mention anything specific to Hinduism, Buddhism, Christianity, Judaism or any other religion. It doesn't mention God, Truth, or Cosmic Consciousness. When it comes time to define practice, Patanjali demonstrates the universality of Yoga by presenting steadiness of mind as *the foundation* of spiritual practice.

That's why it's not a stretch to say that when a Catholic prays the rosary, she or he is essentially performing what the *Yoga Sutras* define as Yoga practice. The same is true for a Buddhist monk practicing walking meditation in Thailand, a Jew praying at the Western Wall, or a Muslim facing Mecca in prayer. They may or may not know the name, "Yoga," but according to the *Yoga Sutras*, the authority on the subject, they are engaged in Yoga practice. It's not that they derived their practices from Hindu mystical traditions. These principles and practices are anchored in a universal dimension and are rediscovered in every age and place.

The practices presented in the *Yoga Sutras* can be placed in the following categories:

- Moral and ethical precepts, the *yamas* and *niyamas* (see the *Sanskrit Glossary*).
- The physical practices of asana (postures) and pranayama (breathing practices) as a preparation for meditation.
- Sense regulation (pratyahara) and the progressively deeper states of meditation (dharana, dhyana, samadhi).
- Discriminative discernment (*viveka*). The ability to discern the changing from the changeless, the pleasurable from the beneficial, the impure from the pure, and the non-Self from the Self.
- Understanding and accepting suffering as an aid for helping to eliminate the limitations of spiritual ignorance (*tapas*).

- Study (*svadhyaya*) of the self, sacred texts, Nature, and the repetition of mantras.
- Devotion to God or self-surrender (*Ishwara Pranidhanam*).

All Yoga practices are performed against the backdrop of nonattachment (vairagya). Nonattachment allows every practice to fully flourish, while the practices help develop nonattachment.

Practice becomes firmly grounded when well tended for a long time, without break, and with enthusiasm. 1.14.

A firmly grounded practice is one that occurs daily, without strain or grudging participation. It is meaningful, inspired, and focused. It is a joyful habit that accompanies you throughout your life and becomes the unbroken thread that guides you to Self-realization. It is an anticipated time of connection to deeper levels of your mind, of discovery and nurturance, and of integration and wholeness. This vision of practice is the ideal and is attained by anyone who follows the advice presented in this sutra:

Long time. Success in any worthwhile endeavor requires time; and concerning achieving deep, steady meditation, a long time. How much time depends on past activities, temperament, and current environment. But, the chief factors that determine how long it takes for practice to become firmly grounded are regularity and enthusiasm.

We need to have patience to be successful meditators. No one would expect to become a surgeon, musician, or pilot quickly. Why would it be different with meditation? Stay focused on your goal, but not obsessed with it. It will come.

Without break. To attain success, a long time is not enough. The practice needs to be regular. There is no lack of meditators who wonder why they are not much better off now than ten years ago. If you question them, you'll often find that though they have been practicing for years, their practice has been an on-and-off affair. Progress cannot be made without regularity.

No effort in meditation is wasted. Every mantra repeated, every mindful deep breath, each occasion of dedicated service to others, every prayer, act of worship, affirmation, or bit of sacred knowledge learned, adds to the momentum and depth of practice.

With enthusiasm. Years of regular practice still might not produce the expected results if it is not done with an attitude that is conducive to success. Meditation flourishes when practiced with enthusiasm, sincerity, and love. Enthusiasm is the key to being able to practice for a long time and without break.

The promise of benefits serves as the inspiration in the beginning. Later, the peace and joy of the Self dawning on the mind becomes the great motivator.

Anyone who practices faithfully and diligently will get the results. There's no doubt about it. We develop into better people, looking within to find the devotion, consistency, and love that are natural to us.

How can you tell if your practice has become firmly grounded? One simple answer is when it is harder *not* to practice than to practice. Another touchstone is when, for reasons beyond your control, practices are missed. Does skipping a day or two, or a change of schedule initiate a tidal wave of irregularity? If so, the practice is not yet firmly grounded. Those who have grounded their practice are not thrown off by changes in schedule, place, or time. For them, the joy and benefits of the practices are stronger than worldly distractions.

Dedicated practice generates a flow of energy towards Self-realization so strong and vital that no other result can follow.

Nonattachment is the manifestation of self-mastery in one who is free from craving for objects seen or heard about. 1.15.

This sutra describes a state of mind that is vital not only for success in meditation, but for finding happiness in life. It is the mindset of someone who seeks to avoid *selfish* attachments. Attachment is the mistaken notion that happiness comes from things outside us. It is a narrowness of vision that understands the world in relation to personal desires. Attachments distract our attention from our intentions, cloud judgment, and set us up for suffering.

Note that this sutra asks us to be without *cravings*, not without *objects*. A life of deprivation is not needed to support meditation. Objects don't possess the power to bring suffering *or* happiness. That power belongs to the mind, its expectations, and its restlessness.

Nonattachment, (*vairagya*, literally, "without color") is the ability to experience and respond to life's events with openness, objectivity, and clarity. Nonattachment is not different from unconditional love. Unconditional love only exists where there is empathy, caring, and a willingness to place the welfare of another above our own. We can only love another to the extent that we are not self-centered.

The practice of nonattachment is a powerful support for meditation. Our attachments form the bulk of distracting thoughts. As we grow in nonattachment, meditation becomes much easier.

> Nonattachment is a process of reeducating the mind through:[46]
> - Carefully observing of the limitations of sense satisfaction. It is the cultivation of realistic, healthy relationships with objects and attainments based on recognizing what the world can and cannot offer.
> - Assessing life's attainments regarding their ability to decrease or increase ignorance.
> - Living according to principles that foster spiritual growth, rather than what feels good at the moment.
> - Cultivating an introspective mindset that is aware of the motives behind actions.
> - The redirection of the will when making choices; not by repression of desires, but by turning attention away from selfish actions and toward those that are selfless.
> - Dedicating the fruits of actions to God or humanity.

Still, it's hard to drop the feeling that nonattachment is somehow unnatural; that it rejects human emotions and promotes a dour view of life. As seekers, we sometimes find ourselves caught in a contradiction. We believe that it is unreasonable to expect the world to provide permanent fulfillment. Meanwhile, even as we strive to experience the peace of the Self, we cling to a list of things we *believe* we need to be happy. This contradiction occurs because we habitually attribute the power to confer happiness to objects and attainments. With time and practice, we will experience for ourselves the liberation that nonattachment brings.

When there is nonthirst for even the gunas (constituents of Nature) due to realization of the Self, that is supreme nonattachment. 1.16.

This is the highest manifestation of nonattachment. It is the outcome of the process begun in the previous sutra, which explained

---

[46] The *self-mastery* mentioned in the nonattachment sutra (1.15), refers to exercises such as those in the bulleted list, which are practiced to reduce attachments.

it as a "manifestation of self-mastery," a state that requires effort. When the mind desires something inappropriate, you tell the mind, "No," and it stays away. Although you may be able to free yourself of new temptations, there are still subtle impressions stored in the mind, memories that will tempt you. The cravings that result from subtle impressions are not easily erased.

But, on this level of nonattachment, you don't even think of attaching. Little by little, as the experience of the Self permeates the mind, attachments slip away, until we experience the supreme nonattachment. It is based on having an inner experience so sweet, satisfying, and compelling that there is nothing on the outside that can compete with it. The yogi is completely free from cravings for anything in creation.

The expression of Ishwara is OM. To repeat it in a meditative way reveals its meaning. 1.27. & 1.28.

Ishwara is a Sanskrit term usually translated as Lord or God. It does not refer to any particular name or form. It is more of a generic term. A Christian may regard Jesus as Ishwara, to many Hindus, it is Krishna. The main point is that wherever we perceive Divinity – a transcendent reality that is beyond birth and death, afflictions of any kind, and that is an omniscient guide – *there* is our Ishwara.

These sutras present one of the most recommended forms of meditation in the yogic tradition, mantra repetition, specifically with the mantra, OM. Repeating OM helps us "tune into" the reality of Ishwara. Although only OM is mentioned, by extension, we can include all mantras.[47]

The next five sutras present various meditation techniques the yogi could experiment with. All the sutras begin with the word, "or." You might think of them as "oars" that help you row to your spiritual home.

Or undisturbed calmness is attained when the perception of a subtle sense object arises and holds the mind steady. 1.35.

This sutra refers to subtle meditation experiences. When they happen, we are encouraged, knowing that we are making progress,

---

[47] Since it represents the entire spectrum of vocalizations, OM is the root of all mantras.

that our mind has achieved a measure of steadiness. Yogic tradition gives a few techniques to test the depth of concentration. For example, focusing on the tip of the nose will bring fragrances. Other techniques bring experiences such as nice lights or entrancing sounds.

Or by concentrating on the supreme, ever-blissful Light within. Or by concentrating on a great soul's mind which is totally freed from attachment to sense objects. 1.36 & 1.37.

The first technique is a visualization of a truth. The Light within is a reality. First, you visualize it, then you realize it.

The second technique allows people who are devoted to a spiritual figure to use faith to inspire their practice. If you have a hard time believing that the Supreme Light is within *you*, you can focus on a great spiritual figure who is free of attachments and in whom you perceive the Light. It's the Light that is the ultimate focus of this practice, not the form or personality.

Or by concentrating on an insight had during dream or deep sleep. 1.38.

Did you ever have a dream that seemed more than a dream, that left you feeling uplifted or impacted in significant spiritual way? It could have been a dream in which you were given advice. What you experienced may be real, from the subconscious, or it may be wishful thinking. It doesn't matter as long as it conforms to a true spiritual principle. You can use such a dream as an object of meditation.

In deep sleep, we think that we feel or know nothing. Yet, we know if we slept well. There is a sense of self that is retained even in dreamless sleep. There is an aspect of who we are that doesn't slumber, that is aware even in deep sleep. We also associate deep sleep with a peaceful untroubled state of mind. The peace of deep sleep, and the continuity of self-awareness in dreamless sleep are the objects of meditation suggested in this sutra.

Or by meditating on anything one chooses that is elevating. 1.39.

Yoga gives room for personal choice in objects of meditation. You are free to choose any object as long as it inspires you, you have faith in it, and you like it.

By cultivating attitudes of friendliness toward the happy, compassion for the unhappy, delight in the virtuous, and equanimity toward the nonvirtuous, the mind retains its undisturbed calmness. 1.33

We've discussed quite a few different meditation techniques. The Yoga Sutras also give important, practical advice on how to retain the peace of mediation throughout your daily life. It is nicknamed, The Four Locks and the Four Keys. The locks are the four categories of people and situations we encounter. The keys are the attitudes to employ to ensure that we retain our peace.

Note that the locks and keys don't tell us what to do, but what attitude ensures a clear, objectivity. With that state of mind, we are in the best position to make a proper assessment of choices of actions.

This sutra prompts us to cultivate a higher vision of life: to see and make friends with happiness, to have compassion wherever we see suffering, to celebrate the joy of a virtue, and to remember that no one is well served if we allow negative thoughts and actions to extinguish our inner peace.

This is one sutra worth memorizing. It will be an invaluable guide. Also, keep in mind to apply the Locks and Keys to yourself.

2.29. The eight limbs of Yoga are:
1. **yama (abstinence): nonviolence, truthfulness, nonstealing, continence, nongreed**
2. **niyama (observance): purity, contentment, accepting pain as a help for purification, study, and worship of God (self-surrender)**
3. **asana – posture**
4. **pranayama – breath control**
5. **pratyahara – sense withdrawal**
6. **dharana – concentration**
7. **dhyana – meditation**
8. **samadhi – contemplation, absorption or superconscious state**

In Yoga, meditation is part of a holistic approach to experiencing Self-realization. This sutra presents what is known as the Eight Limbs of Yoga (*ashtanga yoga*) and forms the core of Yoga practice. They are not steps to be completed one at a time before going on. They represent a harmonious balance and integration of body, mind, and spirit. Patanjali explains that the benefits of practicing these limbs is that they awaken our inner wisdom and confer the discriminative discernment necessary to overcome ignorance.

Yamas and Niyamas. These moral and ethical precepts are considered the foundation of yogic life. The yamas are guidelines that should be followed by anyone, regardless of who they are, what they do, where they are, or circumstances. Because of this the are called *mahavratam*, great vows. The niyamas are principles that should be part of the daily practice of Yoga students.

Don't think of them simply as rules. That would drain them of their life and ultimate benefits. They are ways of seeing life. The yamas and niyamas are what life looks like through the eyes of the enlightened. Practicing them is not so much about learning what to do or not do, but how to see. The yamas and niyamas help us awaken. Try choosing one yama or niyama per week to focus on.

In the list that follows, the first five principles are the yamas, and the next five, the niyamas.

- Nonviolence (*ahimsa*). This is supreme among all the yamas, never to be violated. We should not knowingly cause harm to human beings, animals, and so-called inanimate objects in thought, word, and deed. Ahimsa, like most moral and ethical precepts, challenges us to have our beliefs, motives, and actions in alignment.
- Truthfulness (*satya*). When we live this principle, we become integrated human beings. Our thoughts, words and deed agree with the facts. Truthfulness is also about being straightforward with ourselves and others.
- Nonstealing (*asteya*). This yama is a warning not to let the emotion of envy overpower our good sense. Envy can make us jealous, restless, and unhappy. If we don't moderate these feelings, we may be prompted to take what is not ours. The opposite of this is the niyama, contentment.
- Continence (*brahmacharya*). Brahmacharya teaches us to use our energy wisely.
- Yogis should be moderate in all activities. Because the sex act uses so much energy (especially in men), this yama is sometimes translated as celibacy.
- Nongreed (*aparigraha*). This yama is an attitude, not an action. It bespeaks of a basic craving, an unsatisfied state of mind. An

unexamined and unchecked longing to have more of an object, experience, or attainment can lead to vices.
- Purity (*saucha*). This refers to purity on the physical and mental levels. We are encouraged regulate what goes into the body and mind and to engage in practices that cleanse the body of toxins and the mind of unproductive ways of thinking.
- Contentment (*santosha*). Contentment is the ability to live in the present moment.
- Every moment holds the information, guidance, and support we need to succeed…and grow spiritually. It has been said that God is either "now here," or "nowhere."
- Accepting pain as a help for purification (*tapas*). This niyama asks us to recognize and accept life's inevitable occurrences of pain. Instead of striking out in fear, anger, or resentment, we look to such challenges as opportunities for growth. Pain and suffering, more powerfully than anything else, bring our shortcomings into bold relief.
- Study (*svadhyaya*). Yogis should be informed seekers. The teachings help keep us on track in a strong, purposeful, and balanced way.
- Worship of God, self-surrender (I*shwara pranidhanam*). Self-surrender is the willing dedication of time, energy, and abilities to a person, cause, or achievement in hopes of creating a greater reality. Worship of God is not just about ritual and prayer. It means to fully give ourselves to the pursuit of experiencing the highest good, wisdom, and harmony.

Asana and Pranayama. These limbs are preparations for meditation and ways to still the body and regulate the life force.

Sense regulation (*pratyahara*). The fifth limb is concerned with steadying the mind through regulation of the senses. Become mindful of how you use the senses in ways that are not conducive to your health and peace. Engage the senses in activities that produce positive states of mind, but don't strengthen cravings. Learn to enjoy the taste of simply prepared natural foods and good quality entertainment, for example. You can also "fast" from certain objects or activities for a while. If you eat tasty, but not so healthy, fast food every day, try staying away from it one or two days a week. As you become free of that habit, you will gain some mastery over the senses.

Concentration (*dharana*), Meditation (*dhyana*), and Absorption (*samadhi*).
The last three limbs represent the stages of meditation (see sutras 3.1 - 3.3 below) and are the essential subject matter of this text.

When disturbed by negative thoughts, opposite – positive – ones should be thought of. This is *pratipaksha bhavana*. 2.33.

Although this is given as advice for handling difficult situations in life, it can also be understood as a fundamental technique for advancing in meditation. When applying this sutra to meditation, negative thoughts are any that distract attention, and the opposing thought is the object of meditation.

Pratipaksha bhavana emphasizes that meditation is not a forceful suppression of unwanted thoughts, but a continued, gentle, refocusing of attention on the object of meditation.

Thereafter (after mastering asana), one is undisturbed by dualities. 2.48.

One of the main reasons why the practice of Hatha Yoga developed was to address how bodily health and discomfort affect meditation. Progress is more easily made when we can forget the body, allowing the focus to move more deeply within.

We are also reminded of the importance of cultivating a comfortable, steady posture (asana) for meditation.

Dharana (concentration) is the fixing of attention to one place, object, or idea. Dhyana (meditation) is the continuous flow of awareness toward that object. Samadhi (absorption) is the same meditation when the mind, as if giving up its own form, reflects the object alone. 3.1 - 3.3.

First, the mind attempts to fix attention on the object of meditation (*dharana*).

As the same meditation deepens, it is marked by an effortless, steady flow of attention (*dhyana*) toward the object of meditation. The mind is peaceful, clear, and one-pointed, though it will still wander after a while. When that happens, you've slipped back to dharana. With practice, the periods of dhyana increase in length. When they become long enough, you attain the first experiences of samadhi, absorption. There are several levels of samadhi according to:

- How completely the mind is absorbed on the object of meditation (how much you lose ego sense).
- How deeply the mind has probed the object (from its gross manifestation to its subtler essences).

Refer to the *Samadhi: Meditation's Finish Line* for more information regarding samadhi.

BHAGAVAD GITA

The Bhagavad Gita, the Song of God, is part of the epic, Mahabharata. Thought by scholars to have been written somewhere between 200 BCE, and 200 CE, it is one of the most important texts in Hinduism and Yoga.

The Gita is a dialogue between Krishna and his disciple, Arjuna, a prince and warrior. The setting is a battlefield, moments before fighting begins. Arjuna, seeing noble men in both armies, forgets that the purpose of this war is to remove his villainous cousins from their illegal reign. Having lost sight of his royal responsibility, he becomes confused and frightened, declaring that he will not fight. In his despair, he turns to Krishna for guidance.

The Bhagavad Gita is an allegory for spiritual life. We are all Arjuna, forgetting that our true purpose is to overcome challenges in the battlefield of life, conquer ignorance, and find victory in Self-realization.

Like the Yoga Sutras, the Gita presents a holistic approach to spirituality, integrating selfless service (Karma Yoga), study and self analysis (Jnana Yoga), devotion (Bhakti Yoga), and meditation. Following are some selections especially pertinent to meditation.

Equanimity of mind is Yoga. Do everything Arjuna, centered in that equanimity. Renouncing all attachments, you'll enjoy an undisturbed mind in success or failure. 2.48

When your mind, which has been tossed about by conflicting opinions, becomes still and centered in equilibrium, then you experience Yoga. 2.53

There is neither wisdom nor meditation in an always-changing mind. Without a meditative, one-pointed mind, there is no peace. Without peace of mind, how can anyone be happy? 2.66

As you gain control of your mind with the help of your higher Self, your mind and ego become your allies. But the uncontrolled mind behaves as an enemy. 6.6

More than outside circumstances, misperceptions are the cause of pain and suffering. On the other hand, a mind that has attained tranquility, clarity, and focus, is a reliable guide and best friend.

As you gain control of your mind, with the help of your higher Self... reminds us that the deepest part of who we are is available to help us. It is like the ever-blowing wind. We just need to unfurl our sail to make use of it. Meditation is one way to do this.

With a self-disciplined mind, you experience a state of constant serenity, correctly identifying with your highest Self who remains unaffected in heat or cold, pleasure or pain, praise or blame. 6.7

To practice meditation, fix up a clean meditation place with your seat neither too high nor too low. Insulate the seat with a grass mat, then a deerskin, and over those, a clean cloth. 6.11

It's not a requirement that you assemble a meditation seat with grass and a deerskin. The important point is to insulate the body from cold and dampness and from the magnetic force of the Earth that draws our subtle energies downward. You can use wool, cotton, or any natural fiber as part of your meditation seat.

Then sit and calm the mind and senses by concentrating on one thing. Thus you practice meditation for self-purification. 6.12

Keep the body, head, and neck erect without looking about. Gaze instead toward the tip of your nose. 6.13

You don't need to take the instruction to gaze at the tip of the nose literally. The Sanskrit, *nasika-agra*, can also mean root of the nose. It implies that you can focus on the third eye area (between the eyebrows, in the center of the head).

The point is to have the body properly aligned and keep the eyes steady and not looking about. When the gaze is steady, the mind becomes still and focused.

When you have your mind well trained so it rests solely in the Self, without wanting anything, then you are established in Yoga. 6.18

Completely let go of all selfish desires and expectations. Then with your mind, you can withdraw the senses from all sides. 6.24

Little by little your mind becomes one-pointed and still, and you can focus on the Self without thinking of anything else. 6.25

However your mind may wander, continue to draw it back again to rest in the True Self. 6.26

As your mind becomes harmonized through Yoga practices, you begin to see the Self in all beings and all beings in your Self; you see the same Self everywhere and in everything. 6.29

This verse shows the all encompassing nature of enlightenment and why it results in the highest compassion. The entire universe is experienced as Self.

Krishna, you say that equanimity of mind is Yoga. But I do not see how that is possible, because the mind by nature is constantly changing. Not only is it restless, it is often turbulent and powerfully obstinate. Trying to control the mind is like trying to control the wind. 6.33 - 34

Arjuna gives a description of the typical state of mind: restless and constantly changing. Not only that, it is turbulent and powerfully obstinate! The mind *is* as difficult to control as the wind – more so.

The wind is a good analogy. Though we can experience the effects of wind, it remains invisible and mysterious. We are accustomed to the animated graphics of weather forecasts that show where the wind is coming from and where it will go. It's a bit misleading. We don't really know where the wind started and we can't control it. It comes and goes as it pleases, healing or hurting as it travels around the globe. In these ways, the wind is much like the mind.

Then Krishna said: O mighty Arjuna, undoubtedly the mind is restless and very difficult to control. But with steady practice and nonattachment, it can be controlled. 6.35

Note that this is the same advice given in the *Yoga Sutras*. 1.12.

Success in Yoga is extremely difficult if you cannot control your mind. But if you persist and control your mind and earnestly strive for realization using the right methods, you will certainly be successful. 6.36

Is it difficult to attain perfect stillness and clarity of mind? Yes. Impossible? Not at all. Regular, mindful practice takes stillness of mind from a potential, to a probability, to an inevitability.

HATHA YOGA PRADEEPIKA

The *Hatha Yoga Pradeepika* was composed between 1350 and 1400 CE. Although its focus is on the physical practices, it presents Yoga as a holistic science, including quite a bit regarding meditation and Raja Yoga.

I consider those practitioners who only do Hatha Yoga, without knowing Raja Yoga, to be laboring fruitlessly. 4.79

The *Hatha Yoga Pradeepika* presents Hatha Yoga as a means to strengthen and purify the body so that practices, such as meditation, can be practiced with greater success.

Without thought of the external, or even the internal thought. Abandon all thoughts, don't think of anything. 4.57
In meditation, distinctions between impressions that enter the mind from sense stimulation and those that arise from subconscious impressions, evaporate. Meditation helps us transcend relativities.

The entire universe is just the creation of thought. It is a play of mind created by thought. By transcending the mind which is composed of conceptions and thought, peace will definitely be attained, O Rama! 4.58
What we usually experience as a concrete reality is in truth, a combination of an external stimulus (object person, or event) mixed with personal impressions of it. The thing in and of itself remains largely unknown. Our understanding of life, who we are, and the world we live in is composed of such conceptions (vrittis). Ultimately, reality collides with our conceptions of reality with suffering the usual outcome. When we transcend these conceptions, peace is ours.

There are many various methods, depending on individual experience, of the path to enlightenment, as taught by great souls. 4.63
This is the same teaching presented in the *Yoga Sutras*. We are free to choose any object or path of meditation as long as it's uplifting and we like it.

The state in which the individual self and the Supreme Self are experienced as one, in which all thoughts disappear, is called samadhi. 4.7

UPANISHADS

The Upanishads ("to sit near devotedly")[48] are a collection of wisdom texts, with ten considered the most important. Dating back some 2700 years, they are revered as an illumination of *vedanta*, the school of nondualism, considered the highest philosophical knowledge.

The essential teachings of the Upanishads have been distilled to four sayings, the *mahvakyas*, great utterances. They appear below in English and Sanskrit, followed by the source text.

Consciousness is Brahman: Prajnanam Brahma, Aitareya Upanishad.
This Self is Brahman: Ayam Atma Brahma, Mandukya Upanishad.
I am Brahman: Aham Brahmasmi, Brihadaranyaka Upanishad.
Thou art That: Tat Twam Asi, Chandogya Upanishad.

These sayings summarize the essential spiritual truths. Any or all can be used as objects of meditation.

The Upanishads have much to say about meditation. Here is a taste:

Katha Upanishad

When all the senses are stilled, when the mind is at rest, when the intellect wavers not--then, say the wise, the highest state is reached. This calm of the senses and mind has been defined as Yoga. He who attains it is freed from delusion. 2.6.10-11

Svetasvatara Upanishad

Be seated, holding the body steady, with the head, neck, and chest erect. With the senses and mind turned within, you enter into the heart. Thus, the wise cross over the dread sea of birth and death. 2.8.

The heart can be taken as a suggestion to focus on the heart chakra, or it can mean to turn the awareness away from the sights, sounds, and cares of the outside world and toward the core of our being.

The sea of birth and death (reincarnation) is dreaded, because each time we depart from the physical body, we vacate the vehicle we have become attached to, the instrument we believed would carry us to happiness. It is our attachment to people and objects, and to

---

[48] The word is evocative of the guru/disciple relationship, the traditional method for the transmission of sacred knowledge.

sense stimulation and cravings that cause us to dread death. For the enlightened, there is no more coming and going; she or he enjoys the bliss of permanent union with the Self.

Train your senses to be obedient and regulate your activities to lead you to the goal.

With your breath subtle and calm, hold the reins of your mind as you hold the reins of restless horses. 2.9.

While there should never be strain or forcing in the practice of meditation, there *is* effort, enthusiasm, and firm intent. Hold onto the reins of the mind and purposefully turn your attention within to attain the goal.

Choose a place for meditation that is clean, quiet and cool, a cave with a smooth floor, without stones and dust, protected against wind and rain and pleasing to the eye. 2.10.

No cave? No problem.

Arrange a clean, uncluttered space in your home. A cluttered space "crowds" awareness.

Once the mind gets used to going within, it doesn't matter where you are, you can make the mind still and serene anywhere.

YOGA AND RELIGION

Is Yoga a religion? It's a reasonable question. Students can be confused about it. They read or are told that Yoga is not a religion, yet, when they walk into their local Yoga studio, they often see an altar with Hindu deities on it and are treated to chanting the names of deities, such as Ganesh or Durga.

If Yoga is not a religion, is it a way of life, or a science? The answer is not so simple. We first have to define what we mean by religion.

The Latin root of the word, religion, is *religare*, to bind back to. The word is used by different people to refer to different realities. Even scholars and theologians don't agree on a definition of religion. For most of us, the word immediately brings up ideas of a Supreme Being. Yet, there are faith traditions,[49] like Buddhism and Taoism, that have no such ideas. Even so, most people still consider them religions. To understand what religion is, we need to look beyond the usual notions.

Human beings have always tried to make sense of the world they live in. They pondered over unseen forces that determined vital aspects of their lives such as climate, reproduction, and disease. They believed (as we do today) that if they understood these forces, they might be able to control, influence, or cooperate with them to their benefit. They were looking to minimize suffering by avoiding the unexpected and troublesome. In other words, they wanted to be happy.

In their quest to uncover universal laws, some thinkers explored the nature of the cosmos and the world around them. The same explorations continue today as such sciences as biology, astronomy, and physics.

Others looked within for answers to the mysteries of life. Their focused inquiries brought them glimpses of life that transcended the ever-changing world of Nature. In those moments, their concerns slipped away and they enjoyed a taste of something eternal, a timeless state that tied together all aspects of life – a point of ultimate harmony.

The paths of outer and inner explorations are not incompatible; they are complementary. They investigate the same Reality from different viewpoints. The common ground of science and spirituality is the search for the universal laws that govern life.

---

[49] See *faith* and *faith tradition* in the English Glossary.

This search, and the truths it revealed, is religion. It is not limited to one faith tradition, but common to them all. With this in mind, we can understand why some spiritual paths are considered religions even though they do not have a belief in a Supreme Being. All of us are seekers, trying to live according to principles that will put our lives in alignment with universal forces.[50] We are trying to *"Go with the flow."*

If you define religion in this way, Yoga *is* a religion. If religion is defined as institutions, as organized sects and dogma, then Yoga *is not* a religion. How you answer the question is your decision. Yoga, like religion, is a personal quest to end suffering by direct experience of a transcendent truth that brings supreme peace and that is the point of unity for all objects and events.

The Problem with Words

We can learn a great deal from scholars, institutions, or theologians, but it would be a shame to limit our understanding of Yoga and religion to academic definitions. Especially in matters of Spirit, words can get in the way of understanding. Using words as a journalist or scientist does would deprive the teachings of their intended meaning. Spiritual truths are often best expressed poetically rather than literally. Poems invite us to enter and participate into the poet's vision. The type of analysis that is suited for science is not appropriate for poetry. It's the same with faith traditions. Only through immersing ourselves in their practices are inner truths revealed. We'll understand the insights that teachings point to when we live, walk, wrestle, and dance with them. Experience is not only the best teacher, it is the only teacher.

Too often, literal views of teachings are used to exclude people. If a person does not fit someone's notion of a "true believer" that person is liable to be considered an outsider, a threat to the status quo.[51] The history of religions is filled with people and nations fighting over *ideas of God*, but when we look at the lives of Self-realized individuals – the prophets, sages, and saints – we find deep agreement on the essentials.

---

[50] These universal principles are called *dharma*, literally, that which holds together (much the same meaning as *religare*, to bind back to).
See *dharma* in the Sanskrit Glossary for more.

[51] A number of great prophets and spiritual figures, like Jesus and Mohammad, who are now revered, were once seen as threats by their contemporaries.

Of course, institutions do provide advantages and benefits. They help preserve a master's teachings and have the resources to extend their good works to many.

A Way of Understanding Yoga and Religion

Perhaps the most accurate way of defining Yoga as it relates to religions is this:

> *What we know by the name of Yoga is the same as the essence of all faith traditions.*

To be considered a house, a building contains certain essential elements: a foundation, walls, a door, and a roof. The number of doors and windows, square footage, the architectural style, and the landscaping can vary.

Similarly, all faith traditions contain the same essence:
- There is one universal, transcendent Truth that is beyond name, form, and thought.
- That Truth, fully present within every individual, can be realized by a pure heart (still, clear mind).
- Purity of heart is attained by leading a selfless, dedicated life.

From Yoga's standpoint, there is no conflict between the teachings and practices of Yoga and the exercise of anyone's faith tradition. When the vast library of Yoga teachings and techniques is distilled, we discover a description of the goal of Yoga that is common sense spirituality; one that would be difficult to argue against:

> *The goal of Yoga is to have an easeful body, a peaceful mind, and lead a useful life.*
> Sri Swami Satchidananda

This definition from my Master, is not only appealing and simple, it is dead-on accurate.

Certainly, there are sects, institutions, theologians, and clergy that would disagree regarding Yoga's universality. We should respect that and not impose our views on others. Followers of any faith tradition, if they go deep into their path, will discover what we call Yoga. No one needs to convert to or from Yoga. There are many paths, but only one Truth.

Yoga and Hinduism

If you look at a textbook of Hinduism, you'll find Yoga listed as one of six schools of philosophy. This might surprise those who only know of Yoga as physical practices, or a way of life with no connection to a faith tradition.

A deeper understanding of what we call Hinduism reveals that it is really something quite different from what we might think. Even its name is misleading. There is no scripture that uses the word. It is not a monolithic school of thought. It has no founder and no equivalent of a pope. Its more correct name is *Sanatana Dharma*, the eternal truth. Its most fundamental principles include the three we discussed as the essence of all faith traditions and adds a fourth.

- There is one universal, transcendent Truth that is beyond name, form, and thought. This Truth permeates every aspect of creation and beyond.
- This Truth, present within every individual, can be realized by anyone.
- The requirements for realization are a clear, tranquil mind, a pure heart, and a dedicated life.
- A person who has experienced that Truth is qualified to guide others on the path that they took.

Examination of the above principles makes it clear that what we commonly refer to as Hinduism is not limited to India, its sacred texts, or its practices. Any teaching that can bring us to the direct experience of the transcendent Truth is accepted and revered in Sanatana Dharma.

As for Yoga's place in Hinduism, it is not incorrect to say that Yoga is the mystical[52] aspect of Sanatana Dharma. Its emphasis is on practice and on a personal experience of the truth of its teachings rather than dogma and ritual.

---

[52] The root of the word *mystic* is from the Greek, *mystes*, meaning initiate, or *myen*, which means to keep the eyes or lips shut. Both roots refer to someone who is actively engaged in their spiritual path. A mystic is that rare seeker who strives to live the teachings and principles of a spiritual tradition. They are interested in experiencing truths, not simply gaining an intellectual grasp of them.

The root, myen, suggests that spiritual truths are difficult to explain to someone who is not an initiate. The masters wouldn't speak much about them, or would speak in parables. Their lips were shut. Then there are those who are entangled in attachments cannot perceive the subtleties of the path. Their eyes were shut.

IS A GURU NECESSARY?

Yoga. Meditation. Gurus. These ideas are linked in the minds of most people. There are three schools of thought on whether or not a guru is necessary. One asserts that a guru is indispensable for anyone who wishes to seriously practice Yoga. Others say a guru is optional, that we are all gurus to each other and ourselves, and can attain the goal of Yoga on our own. Still others believe that a guru is a hindrance, that the guru/disciple relationship encourages a loss of freedom to think and act according to one's conscience. Is a guru necessary to learn and advance in meditation?

Some scholars estimate that the guru/disciple relationship has been a part of Yoga for over 7000 years. Over all those centuries, it is this relationship, not scripture, or institutions, which has been the most trusted method for the study and practice of Yoga. Isn't it true, that even though automated phone systems may be more efficient, you'd rather speak to a person when there's an issue you need to resolve or when you need information? Computers, recorded messages, and books can't empathize. They can't address or adapt to the nuances of the human heart as it experiences the struggles, questions, and successes of daily life. Yogis have relied on a person-to-person transfer of knowledge and wisdom because human beings can attune to each other.

To be clear, you don't need a guru to learn the basics of meditation. There are many fine books, CDs, and classes. Any of these can provide the fundamentals of theory and practice. More than any other time in history, technology allows us to explore, study, and practice spiritual teachings from many traditions and times. With all that information at our fingertips, asking whether the guru/disciple relationship is still relevant makes sense.

Let's define what a guru is. The guru is not a just spiritual teacher, not even an especially wise and gifted one. The guru is someone in whom a seeker perceives the realization of the spiritual goal. For the disciple, the guru is spiritual potential manifested; made palpable. Without living proof that the Self can be realized, spirituality would exist only as theory.

Yoga's theories and practices are valued because they work. A yogi is not satisfied with just studying ideas regarding the highest peace and wisdom. Theory needs to be transformed into personal experience. The most reliable and quickest way to do this is to study with someone who has attained what we seek.

The guru is not just a dispenser of information, but a guide. What would be the easiest way to navigate a city you've never been to? A map or a GPS would work. Directions from a good friend who lived there would be better. Best, is if your friend traveled with you. He or she could share timesaving shortcuts and the secrets to avoiding rush hour traffic. The guru is a spiritual friend who serves the same purpose in spiritual life.

Enlightenment doesn't come easily. The path has famously been described as a razor's edge.[53] The ego is wily and can cause confusion and distress, especially when its inner workings are exposed (as it is in deep meditation). The guru has traveled the distance, has mastered theory and practice, and knows human nature well. For seekers who are stirred to rise above ignorance, egoism, and suffering, if a guru isn't necessary, it's the closest thing to it.

The Master/Apprentice Relationship

The guru/disciple relationship functions like a master/apprentice relationship rather than a teacher/student one. Apprenticing is the form of study most used and valued by advanced students. It is not for those whose wish to learn is lukewarm.

Many years ago, as I was channel surfing, I came across a public television program. On screen were the hands of a guitarist playing a gorgeous and very complex classical piece. I was amazed at his technique, his fluidity and dexterity. Suddenly, off camera, came a commanding, yet reassuring voice,

Stop. You're playing was awkward in that section. Try again.

Clumsy? I wondered. He was fantastic. Being a musician myself at the time, I took a real interest in what was happening.

The guitarist started again. Soon, the off screen voice interjected.

Stop. It's still awkward. Try again.

I couldn't understand how anyone could find fault in the performance. The guitarist began again, and again the same voice

---

[53] This wonderful description of the spiritual path makes it clear that whether you walk *on* the edge of the razor or try to cross over it, the path is tricky and contains difficulties. It is from the *Katha Upanishad: Arise! Awake! Approach the great and learn. Like the sharp edge of a razor is the path, so say the wise. It is hard to tread and difficult to cross.*

interrupted. But this time, the camera panned back to include the man who was speaking. He was an elderly man who held a guitar on his lap. He looked at the first guitarist and said.

Play it like this.

All I could think was, *wow,* now I understand. His performance was an order of magnitude above what I had been hearing.

The first guitarist was the apprentice, himself an internationally respected classical guitarist. The master was Andre Segovia, hailed as the greatest classical guitarist in the world. The program's name, *Master Class.*

Noteworthy was the reaction of the apprentice, his sheer joy at watching and learning from the master.

Apprenticing requires a strong yearning, an "I'll do whatever it takes to grow" attitude, and a degree of humility that is beyond that required of a student.

If you apprenticed with Michelangelo, you might be assigned the task of cleaning his brushes. For months, maybe years, there would be no formal class or even informal advice. You would simply observe the master at work and wash his brushes. There would be no formal class. This lengthy period of observation tests the sincerity and commitment of the apprentice. Deep self-examination becomes an integral part of apprenticing.

Learning through apprenticeship engages the mind on a different level than a classroom setting. The way the mind gains and processes information is different. The mind, so fond of lists and structure, is thrown back on subtler resources. Exquisitely subtle techniques that would resist being reduced to words are relayed in the apprentice relationship. This is the principle of emulation.

There are techniques (and truths) that can't be taught in any conventional sense. These are the skills and capacities that require a "knack" to master. Take for example, working with pizza dough. I used to frequent a local bakery that made fantastic pizza and breads. I got to know Massimo, the baker and owner, well. He learned his trade in Rome by apprenticing with a master baker for many years. I thought it would be fun to buy some dough from him and make my own pizzas at home. He declined, saying that I couldn't possibly work with the dough, since it was so slack (wet and stretchy). I told him I had a lot of experience making my own pizza dough. He invited me into the kitchen. Taking a piece of dough out of a container, Massimo put it on a marble slab and invited me to work with it. No way. I felt like I was caught in a spider's web of sticky dough. It stuck all over my fingers, hands and the marble slab I was working on. As I cleaned myself off, I watched as Massimo took the same dough and quickly, effortlessly, stretched and shaped it into a disk, ready for toppings. "It a knack," he said. "There's no way I can tell you how to do this. You would have to watch for a long time, like I did in Rome." It's the same with many skills, like learning to throw a curve ball, inserting acupuncture needles, or making pottery. The skill, the knack, is learned by observation and emulation. To a large extent the knack, not only for understanding the teachings, but for attaining higher spiritual states, is what the guru/disciple relationship is about.

The Disciple as Empty Cup

There is still another way in which the guru/disciple relationship is not the same as a teacher/student relationship. The premise of the two relationships is different. A student's responsibility is to take in what the teacher gives without editing it. Afterward, they sift through what was taught, keeping what seems useful and putting aside what does not. A disciple approaches the guru as an empty cup. Rather than thinking, "*I know something. I just need to learn something more,*" the disciple's attitude is, "*I've tried to grow spiritually. I realize that I can't do it on my own. Please tell me what to do and I will do it to the best of my ability.*"

The relationship between the guru and disciple is a close one, based on mutual respect. More than anything, it rests on the faith and devotion of the disciple. Gurus don't exist without disciples. No one *is* a guru. No true guru would consider himself or herself to *be* a guru. The guru comes into "existence" only when the student sees the guru in him or her. That is what is meant by the saying, "*When the student is ready, the guru appears.*" The capacity to perceive the Self in another human being marks one of the most significant stages in spiritual life. Seekers who have had that experience have gained the capacity to recognize It, in themselves.[54] It is precisely *because* the guru is a human being that the guru/disciple relationship has such power and efficacy.

---

[54] The word recognize is perfect here. Re - cognize means to know again. The disciple has already sensed the Self within before perceiving it in the guru. If they didn't already catch a glimpse of It within, how could they recognize it in another?

The intensity of devotion shown to gurus by their disciples might seem a little over-the-top to Western observers.[55] Is this intensity reasonable and something beneficial, or are disciples natural born followers yearning to adore and be adored by a father or mother figure, to resolve old familial hang ups?

What the Guru Really Is

Let's take a deeper look at what the guru really is. The guru is not the body, not the mind, not even the intellect. It is the Self, or God, that is the guru. As such, the guru exists within us all. This being true, why is it necessary to have someone else show us the way?

Only a lit candle can light an unlit one. The fire hidden within a stick manifests when it is rubbed against another stick. Similarly, the Truth within is transmitted or called forth by another human being. Books may contain useful information, but they can't teach, guide, or correct misunderstandings. We wouldn't trust surgeons whose education was limited to books. We demand that they have studied and apprenticed with skilled, experienced physicians who oversaw and tested every step of their development. This need for guidance and direction, one human being to another, is even truer in spirituality. The guru/disciple relationship is a process that is part osmosis, part inspiration, part teaching, and part guidance – wrapped in mutual respect and affection.

Initiation

Central to the bond between guru and disciple is initiation, the formal entry into the guru/disciple relationship. It marks the beginning of this relationship and accelerates spiritual growth.

The minute you accept someone as your Guru, you have decided to commit yourself to his or her teaching. That is why only those that are very, very, serious, very interested; those who know the benefit of it, should take initiation.
Sri Swami Satchidananda

---

[55] Yoga is marked by practicality. Western yogis who have adopted some meaningful cultural traditions from India have done so as a help for their growth. Some behaviors, like touching someone's feet as a show of respect and humility, is perhaps a bit unsettling to our eyes. In India, it is quite common, and is even performed by children to their parents and schoolteachers.

At initiation, disciples are typically taught a meditation technique to use. Often, they receive a mantra to repeat as the central part of their daily practices. Yet, there is more to initiation than this.

Disciples receive a transmission of spiritual energy from the guru to help them on their path. It's like a fully charged battery giving current to a weaker one. This transmission of energy is the core of initiation.

Once students receive this energy, they cultivate the charge within themselves by repeating the mantra and following the teachings to the best of their ability. The guru's responsibility is to serve the disciples by guiding them to the experience of Self-realization, regardless of how long it takes.

Committing to a guru/disciple relationship is not something to rush or force. If you are strongly moved to have a guru in your life, that person will appear, though not necessarily right away.

Recognizing the Guru

If you've come across someone you are drawn to, examine his or her teachings and way of being. Talk to disciples. Get a sense for what it's like with their guru. Gurus are individuals. Every guru has a different way of guiding students, a different emphasis and tradition. Some give many talks, others hardly speak, a few don't speak at all. Some are still physically alive, others are not.[56]

Although it is the guru within that recognizes the guru outside, there are a number of factors you can examine before committing to the relationship. The guru should be someone who:

- Demonstrates a deep familiarity with the sacred texts and wisdom of their tradition.
- Is part of a lineage of gurus.
- Shows loving respect for her or his students.
- Puts the welfare of the students before his or her own.
- Is a good example of the teachings.

Of course, the faith and devotion that are part of the guru/disciple relationship has potential pitfalls. Strong emotions and attachments

---

[56] Those whose guru is not in the physical body receive guidance from senior disciples who can serve as spiritual directors, the community of followers (sangha*), and from books, videos, and CDs. Through these, and application of the teachings, they gradually learn to connect with the guru within.

*As is said in the Gospel of Mark, 18.20: *Where two are more gather together as my followers, I am there among them.*

can be involved. The relationship can degenerate into personality worship. These problems may manifest due to a need to find certainty, or to love and be loved unconditionally. There are also less-than-scrupulous "gurus" who become attached to being adored rather than serving their disciples. They can subtly distort teachings to bind students to them. That is why the guru/disciple relationship should not be based on blind faith, but on clear information, self-reflection, enthusiasm, devotion, and love.

The possible pitfalls of the relationship also speak of its inherent power for transformation. The guru/disciple relationship is a proven and potent path for cleaning the ego of selfishness and ignorance.

Yoga has never abandoned the guru/disciple relationship as the foundation of spiritual life. In its long history, there are scriptural warnings against relying on ritual, intellectual learning, philosophy, and of every path of learning, but the guru is *never* dismissed.

To know the Eternal, let the seeker humbly approach a guru devoted to Brahman and well-versed in the scriptures. To a disciple who approaches reverently, who is tranquil and self-controlled, the wise teacher gives, faithfully and without holding back, that knowledge by which is known the truly existing, the changeless Self.
Mundaka Upandishad

The guru is the ladder that leads to the rooftop. Once there, we let go of the ladder and get on with the work that needs to be done. The guru is like the telephone that transmits the message, and the mama bird that nudges its offspring out of the nest when it is time for them to fly.

The guru's responsibility is to help you become who you already are. A true guru will take every opportunity to hold up a 'mirror' to you to affirm that, "*Whatever you see in me that inspires and uplifts you, is your own Self.*"

If after careful investigation, you find someone in whom you have faith, don't hesitate. If you are not completely sure, it's always better to wait. If you don't see the need for a guru for yourself, it's still worthwhile to find someone more experienced than you who can serve as a mentor. Dethroning the selfish ego from its ensconced perception that it is the center of the universe is not so easy.

EXPLORE MORE

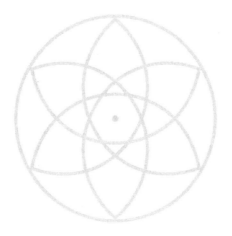

THE THREE FACULTIES OF THE MIND
MANAS, BUDDHI, AHAMKARA

In Yoga, the mind is referred to as the *chitta* (from the root *cit*, to know). The chitta is composed of three faculties: *manas*, *buddhi*, and *ahamkara*.

Manas is the aspect of mind that records data. It receives input from the environment and from the subconscious and presents it to...

Buddhi (also called *mahat*), the discriminative faculty. The buddhi compares and contrasts incoming data with existing mental impressions to make sense of it and integrate it in a useful way. The buddhi is also understood as the cosmic aspect of the intellect. As the first expression of Prakriti (primordial Nature), it can best reflect the Self, and is able to grasp intuitive insights.

Ahamkara is the sense of ego. It is the feeling of individuality, of "I and me." The ego declares mental impressions as it own, creating the individual mind. What we call a mind is just a bundle of thoughts claimed by the ego. Functionally, the ego stands between manas and buddhi. It can choose to affiliate more closely with the sense oriented consciousness of manas or the higher discriminative functions of buddhi. Since it serves as a channel for the Self, affiliating with the buddhi opens us to wisdom and intuitive guidance. The difference between a life that leads to liberation and a life bound by ignorance is just a simple tilting of the mind toward or away from the buddhi. Meditation tilts manas towards the buddhi.

Considering the above functions of the mind, it might be surprising to learn that the mind does not have consciousness as an intrinsic property. Its awareness is "borrowed" from the Self. *Patanjali's Yoga Sutras* give three philosophical proofs that the mind has no consciousness of its own (*sutras* 4.19 - 21).

- The mind can be perceived by the Self. If the contents and activities of the mind can be observed, it cannot be the seat of consciousness.
- The mind can't be aware of its own contents and external objects at the same time.
- If we postulate that individual consciousness is based on one part of the mind watching another, we have to contend with the question: *How do I know that one part of my mind is watching another?*

There must be a third aspect of the mind that is watching the watcher, and a fourth to watch the third. Thought process and memory would be reduced to a shambles. Where would we store memories, and how could we access them?

The mind is subtle matter, a reflection of the Self (pure consciousness) on Nature (*Prakriti*). Although consciousness itself is never limited, it seems to be due to its association – its reflection – on matter. What is born from this relationship is individual consciousness. If we compare the Self to the sun and Nature to a mirror, we can say that the sun, unthinkably larger than a mirror, is not limited by its reflection on it.

THE ROOT OF ALL OBSTACLES

The Yoga Sutras of Patanjali lists five obstacles (*klesas*, afflictions). They are the root cause of all suffering and affect everyone.

Ignorance, egoism, attachment, aversion, and clinging to bodily life are the five obstacles. 2.3.

These obstacles function on a deeper level than those addressed earlier in the *Sutras*.[57] Called *klesas*, afflictions, they are like a genetic disorder that plagues human beings throughout their lives.

Ignorance is the root of all the klesas. If our true nature is peace and joy, then what else but ignorance can be the cause of suffering? We forget that we are the Self and think that we are the body/mind. This fundamental misperception sets off a chain reaction of obstacles that cause endless distress.

Egoism is the first result of ignorance. With the appearance of egoism, the peace and fulfillment of the Self is forgotten. We mistakenly believe that we are just a mind encased in a body whose life span and opportunities for happiness are limited. This causes the mind to become restless. It begins to search for happiness and meaning in possessions, position, and sense experiences.

The ego forms attachments to things or circumstances that have brought pleasure. We become accustomed to searching for externals for happiness.

The brother of attachment is aversion; the avoidance of anything we believe will bring pain.

We cling to life in the body since it is the medium through which the mind (via the sense organs) experiences the pleasure we seek.

The klesas are reminiscent of the notion of original sin in Christianity. Adam and Eve were enjoying communion with God and an idyllic life in the Garden of Eden. God's only instructions were that the land be cultivated and that Adam should not eat the fruit of the Tree of Knowledge of Good and Evil, *"for the day that you eat from it, you will surely die."* (Genesis 2.17) Let's compare the Biblical teachings with the klesas:

The *knowledge* referred to in the Bible is the same as the *ignorance* spoken of in Yoga. They are two ways to refer to the same experience.

---

[57] *Chitta vikshepa*, the shaking of the mind, sutra 1.30.

Adam and Eve gained knowledge of their individuality, but lost, or became ignorant of, knowledge of God.

"Good and evil" is analogous to attachment (we perceive as good that which brings pleasure) and aversion (we perceive as bad that which brings pain).

In the Bible, God tells Adam if he eats this particular fruit, he will die. In other words, if he identifies himself with his finite body/mind, he will forget the reality of his immortal nature and experience fear of death. This is comparable to clinging to bodily life.

Just as all humans become heir to ignorance, the sin of Adam and Eve is considered the inheritance for all humanity. Whether we call it ignorance or original sin, we are talking about that which alienates us from the experience of the Self.

STILLNESS REDEFINED

Most meditation instruction includes words like still, focused, one-pointed, unwavering, and fixed. These terms are all useful if properly understood. They may also give the false impression that meditation is a practice in which the ultimate goal is a static state in which there is no movement or change in individual consciousness. This misunderstanding can lead to difficulties, especially as meditators advance in their practice. Approaching meditation with the notion that the mind must be stifled, leads to tension and a subtle strengthening of the ego that obstructs progress and disturbs peace of mind.

Both the mind and the object of meditation are matter, part of Nature. As such, it is their nature to change and evolve. In meditation, neither the mind nor the object of meditation is static. The mind links with the object of meditation[58] through prolonged attention. The mind and the object take a journey together in which increasingly subtle facets of both are revealed.

The notion that the mind must be static in meditation can be traced to difficulties in translating key terms from Sanskrit. It's always tricky rendering words from one language to another. Historical and cultural contexts are often missing or vague.[59] Our language also doesn't have words that precisely capture the fullness and nuances of many of the key principles and practices of Yoga. In India, the nature of the mind and consciousness have been the focus of intense introspective study, analysis, and experimentation for thousands of years. Words were coined and used in ways that have no exact English equivalent. N*irodha* is one such term. It is usually translated as something like restraint or restriction. E*kagrata*, another important word used in explaining meditation, is translated as one-pointed. The translations are not incorrect, but they don't have the subtleties that give the Sanskrit terms life and three dimensionality. Let's take a fresh look at the concepts of restraint and one-pointedness.

Our usual waking awareness is marked by what we might call horizontal (or lateral) awareness. Our attention continually, often

---

[58] The yoking (yoga) of the mind to an object of meditation is a classic definition of the word yoga.

[59] When General Electric was establishing itself in China decades ago, it faced a problem when the word-for-word translation of their motto, "GE, we bring good things to life," came out terribly twisted, "GE, we bring your ancestors back from the dead."

restlessly, shifts between objects, and from objects to sensations, desires, memories, and back again. It's something like channel surfing. We don't tend to stay very long with any program. As one comedian joked, "We're not so much interested in what's on, but what *else* is on."

There is little depth of understanding in horizontal awareness. Fuller and subtler aspects of the object of attention are not revealed since the mind soon flits to something else. If we meet twelve people at a party, we might learn a dozen names, faces, and occupations, but very little else.

As we practice meditation, the lateral movement of awareness is gradually restrained (nirodha). Little by little, the vrittis (the thought-amalgams through which we perceive life) begin to untangle as awareness focuses on an individual thought (the object of meditation).

As the mind becomes steadier in focus and clarity, the horizontal movement ends and the mind changes direction, so to speak. Awareness still moves, but its movement now shifts vertically, going deeper within. Subtler layers of consciousness are plumbed.[60] The mind becomes absorbed in these subtler realities, and insights spontaneously arise (*prajna*).

The mind continues its dive into consciousness until the ego sense (*ahamkara*) is encountered in its purest, most naked form. All there is in this state is awareness of "I." At this point we begin to experience another significant change in consciousness. Arising and subsiding and thought-waves are identical (ekagrata, one-pointed). Note that, even though this state is referred to as one-pointed, there is still movement.

At this point, the conscious mind has been completely probed and understood, but subconscious impressions remain. As the meditation deepens, even the subconscious impressions become inactive, and we finally attain stillness of mind at every level.[61]

Meditation is a progressive undertaking in which the mind is not riveted to stillness, but united with the object of meditation. Together, the object and our attention travel within, revealing subtler aspects of each other, and leading us to stillness.

It is noteworthy that, in the end, stillness only comes when we abandon effort and allow the Self to embrace us. Absorbed in that

---

[60] See sutra 1.17 in the *Samadhi* section of this book.
[61] See *nirodha* in the *Sanskrit Glossary*.

embrace, the false notion of separateness dissolves. This is Yoga, union. Ignorance and the suffering it brings, is transcended by a stunning paradox: you find your Self only when you lose your self. This is what Jesus meant when he said that we have to die to be reborn.[62] It is also the same as the Buddha's nirvana, the state where all conceptions of self and the universe are extinguished.

This gives birth to a radical, but entirely natural state of being, a dual consciousness, a constant awareness of the oneness of all creation while simultaneously enjoying the differences (perceiving the unity in diversity). This state has been called *sahaja samadhi*, the natural, organic samadhi, the "eyes wide open samadhi."

---

[62] John, 3.3

YOGA AND EMOTIONS

Yogic teachings usually refer to emotions as two general states of mind: agitated or steady.

The agitated state consists of thoughts that are ignited by selfish attachment. These thoughts are associated with a desire for pleasure (security, happiness, prestige, comfort) or avoidance of pain. In this category we find such emotions as anger, fear, lust, and greed. We also experience an excited happiness that results from fulfilling desires. Agitated emotions, whether we regard them as positive or negative, tilt consciousness away from objectivity and clarity. These emotions indicate a mind that perceives itself as a discrete entity, completely separate from others and Nature.

Clear, calm awareness also has emotions associated with it, but these emotions are considered qualities of the Self reflecting on the mind. Here you will find emotions such as joy, peace, compassion, and selfless love. These emotions speak of the experience of harmony and unity.

Yoga psychology is not limited to analyzing or controlling emotions, but on cultivating those that are associated with a clear, selfless state of mind. These powerful emotions don't cause harm, and are strong enough to overcome the negative ones.

A regular practice of meditation will help balance and strengthen positive emotions. However, for those that have deep-seated trauma or complex emotional problems, while meditation can greatly aid healing, counseling is often indicated.

MEDITATION AND THE BRAIN
A LITTLE SCIENCE

The Prefrontal Cortex and The Amygdala ... The Sage vs. The Incredible Hulk

Studies suggest that meditation affects the relationship between the amygdala and the prefrontal cortex. The amygdala is the part of the brain that reacts quickly, without reflection. As the center of fear memories, it can often lead to impulsive reactions of anger or anxiety. In contrast, the prefrontal cortex is the part of the brain that pauses to think and consider before acting. Because of this, it is also known as the inhibitory center.

Though the prefrontal cortex is very good at analyzing and planning, it takes a relatively long time to make decisions (not useful in emergencies). The amygdala, on the other hand, is simpler (and older in evolutionary terms). It makes rapid judgments about a situation and therefore has a powerful effect on emotions and behaviors that are linked to survival needs. For example, if a gorilla leaps out of your bedroom closet, the amygdala will trigger a fight or flight response long before the prefrontal cortex responds.

While useful in emergencies, the amygdala is prone to error, such as seeing danger where there is none. This is particularly true in contemporary society where social conflicts are far more common than encounters with predators. A harmless, but emotionally charged situation can trigger uncontrollable fear or anger, leading to conflict, anxiety, and stress.

There is roughly a quarter of a second gap between the time an event occurs and the time it takes the amygdala to react. In that fleeting moment, a skilled meditator may be able to intervene before a fight or flight response takes over, and perhaps redirect the mind to more constructive or positive feelings.

Some studies have linked meditation to increased activity in the left prefrontal cortex, which is associated with concentration, planning, meta-cognition (thinking about thinking), and positive, happy feelings. There are similar studies linking depression and anxiety with decreased activity in the same region, and/or with dominant activity in the right prefrontal cortex. Meditation increases activity in the left prefrontal cortex, and the changes are stable over time. Even if you stop meditating, the effect lingers.

Can Compassion Change Your Brain?

Some recent studies suggest that we can train ourselves to be compassionate. Cultivating compassion through meditation affects regions of the brain that can make a person more empathetic to other peoples' mental states.

MRI studies have shown that positive emotions such as lovingkindness and compassion can be learned in the same way as playing a musical instrument or gaining basic skills in a sport. The scans revealed that the brain circuits that are used to identify emotions and feelings were significantly changed in people who were experienced practitioners of Buddhist compassion meditation.

Peace chants and affirmations such as those that are presented in this book can also encourage these changes if done on a regular basis and in a focused, heartfelt manner.

The implications of this are amazing. Imagine a world where it is common knowledge that empathy could be developed through attentive awareness on compassionate thoughts and images. The benefits to families, communities, and governments would be incredible. We would live in a world of better parents, teachers, healers, and friends. Happiness and peace would increase while depression, envy, and lust would decrease.

About Brain Waves

The science of brain waves is the study of the rhythm of the brain during different activities. Brain cells, called neurons, communicate with each other through electrical impulses, generating these rhythms.

Brain waves are measured in Hertz (Hz). The lower the number, the slower the brain activity. The categories of brain waves are associated with different states of consciousness.

Beta waves (15-30 Hz, or waves, per second). This is the brain rhythm of the normal waking state. It is associated with thinking, conscious problem solving, and active attention directed towards the outer world.

Alpha waves (9-14 Hz). In relaxation, brain activity slows from the more rapid patterns of beta into the more gentle waves of alpha. Subjectively, people generally feel more secure, creative, and experience an improved sense of peace and wellbeing. Early stages of meditation are characterized by increased alpha wave activity. It is the gateway that leads into deeper states of consciousness. Alpha waves are also a characteristic of the mind of someone under hypnosis.

Theta waves (4-8 Hz). In deeper meditation, you enter the theta state where brain activity slows almost to the point of sleep. It is a boundary between the conscious state and sleep, a state which we normally only experience fleetingly on waking, or drifting off to sleep.

When theta waves predominate, subconscious memories and activities are more accessible. Theta is more elusive than the alpha state, but it is an extraordinary state of mind. We are receptive to information beyond our normal conscious awareness. Some experts believe that theta meditation awakens intuition and other extrasensory perception skills.

Theta waves can occur during meditation, daydreaming, dreams, creativity, paranormal phenomena, out of body events, and ESP experiences.

Delta waves (1-3 Hz). This slowest of brainwave activity is found during deep, dreamless sleep. It is also sometimes found in very experienced meditators, even when not asleep.

Gamma waves (frequency shifts from 20 to 40 Hz) are involved in higher mental activity. In gamma wave activity, transient periods of synchronized nerve impulses fire over its waveband. Entire banks of neurons from different parts of the brain work together to generate a coherent, concerted cognitive act, such as perception. Recent studies have shown that recognition of new insights occur when frequencies shift from 20 to 40 Hz.

EPILOGUE
Awaken Inside Yoga Meditation

It will happen one day or another; this lifetime or another. One day you will awaken from the illusion that you are a mind encased in a body. You will be embraced by, and absorbed in, the truth of who you are.

You're already there, already one with the essence and source of life. The mystery is how we could have missed this truth and why we resist fully believing it. Are daily cares, responsibilities, and expectations really capable of blotting out the Light of this Truth? Aren't the eyelids, so thin, small, and fragile, capable of blotting out much of the light of the sun from our vision?

In spiritual life, all effort is directed toward one goal: to awaken to who we are through direct experience. As the Self, we experience no lack, no disease or old age, no fear, envy, or stress. There is no competition with others because there are no "others." We are one at the deepest level.

In the end, spiritual life is not about religion, doctrine, or rituals. It's about realizing that our calling is to be happy, to have fun. Fun that has no equal and no opposite. A deep and fulfilling fun that erases doubt, ignorance, and separation.

Why should you meditate? The answer will change your life forever.

It is time to awaken.

OM *Peace, Peace, Peace*

May the entire universe be filled with peace and joy, love and light.

May the Light of Truth overcome all darkness. Victory to that Light!

SANSKRIT GLOSSARY
A

abhyasa – practice. Lit., to apply oneself toward. Continuous endeavor, vigilance, exercise, repetition, exertion. In Yoga, it is paired with vairagya (nonattachment) as the means to enlightenment.

advaita – nondualism; monism, Reality regarded as one and indivisible; beyond pairs of opposites, such as hot/cold, up/down, male/female, good/bad. It is noteworthy that, strictly speaking, the word does not describe the truth, only what that truth is *not*. The highest understanding of Reality is that it is nondual (which is not the same as oneness). It is beyond relativities, and therefore out of the reach of the intellect. By presenting the highest reality in the negative, it resists having the Absolute reduced to a thought-formula.

ahamkara – *kri* = action + *aham* = "I." Lit., *"the I-maker."* Egoism, the sense of individuality.

ahimsa – non-injury. One of the yamas of Raja Yoga.

anahata – the unstruck, the continuous inner humming vibration; the heart chakra.

ananda – bliss, the thing wished for, the end of the drama. The last meaning is noteworthy. Ananda is not just an ordinary happiness, but it is the climax of life, its fulfillment. In the same way that the climax of a drama brings the story to a resolution and is what we came to see, ananda is why we are born.

asamprajnata samadhi – noncognitive samadhi. The state of meditative absorption in which there are no objects in the conscious mind to contemplate. Only subconscious impressions remain.

asana – a steady, comfortable posture. It can refer to the various seated postures used for meditation as well as to the bending and stretching practices of Hatha Yoga.

ashtanga Yoga – refers to the eight limbs of Raja Yoga: yama, niyama, asana, pranayama, pratyahara, dharana, dhyana, samadhi.

asmita – I-am-ness. Another word for the ego sense. In the *Yoga Sutras*, asmita samadhi is the highest of the four levels of absorption in the category of samprajnata samadhi.

EXPLORE MORE: SANSKRIT GLOSSARY

atman – the Self or Brahman when regarded as abiding within the individual.

B

bhakti – devotion. From *bhaj* = to partake of; to turn to.

B*hakti* **Yoga** – the Yoga of devotion to any name and form of the Divine.

B*hagavad* **Gita** – a Hindu scripture, a portion of the epic *Mahabharata* composed 2400 years ago, in which Lord Krishna instructs his disciple Arjuna in various essential aspects of Yoga.

bija – seed, source.

bija mantra – a class of mantras that are often only given through mantra initiation. They are powerful sound formulas that have no translatable meaning.

Brahma – God as creator of the universe. One of the Hindu trinity, which also includes Vishnu and Siva. Note that Brahma is not the same as *Brahman*, the ultimate reality, or *brahmin*, a Hindu priest.

brahmamuhurta – the two-hour period before sunrise that is especially conducive to meditation.

Brahman – greater than the greatest. The unmanifest supreme consciousness or God. In Vedanta, it refers to the Absolute Reality. It is considered *nirguna*, beyond the qualities of nature. It is the highest reality and cannot be conceptualized. Brahman is pure existence, knowledge, and bliss. It is reality whereas the created universe is only an appearance.

buddhi – from the root *budh* to enlighten, to know. Intellect, discriminative faculty of the mind, understanding, reason. (*See mahat.*)

C

chakra – lit., wheel. Refers to any one of seven major centers of consciousness located in the subtle body along the spine.

chit – to perceive, observe, know.

chitta – from *chit*; *see above*. In the *Yoga Sutras*, chitta refers to the mind-stuff. In the nondualistic school of Vedanta (Advaita Vedanta) it refers to the subconscious.

D

darshana – the insight, vision, or experience of an enlightened being; any philosophical school. Yoga is considered one of six orthodox darshanas of Hinduism.

dharana – concentration; the practice of continually refocusing the mind on the object of meditation. The sixth of the eight limbs of Raja Yoga.

dharma – lit., that which holds together. Duty, righteousness, religion, virtue, law, justice, universal law. It is the foundation of all order: religious, social, and moral.

Sri Swami Sivananda defines dharma as that which brings harmony. There are two general classifications of dharma: that which is common to all and that which is specific to a particular class or stage of life. It is further broken down as:

- *varna ashrama dharma*: one's specific duty according to class and stage of life.
- *sanatana dharma*: the Eternal Truth, spirituality based on universal principles. It is the more accurate name for what is now commonly called Hinduism.
- *swadharma*: one's one duty as dictated by inborn talents, traits, etc. One's specific purpose in life.
- *apad dharma*: duties prescribed in times of adversity.
- *yuga dharma*: the laws and codes of conduct appropriate to one's era in time.
- *sadharana dharma*: the general obligations of common duties incumbent on everyone.

Dharma is also one of the Four *Purusharthas*, the four virtuous desires:

- material needs (*artha*): striving to provide you and your family with a home, food, clothing, a retirement fund, and the other needs of life.
- enjoyment (*kama*): enjoyment of the senses. We are here to enjoy life.
- righteousness (*dharma*): duty, righteousness. Dharma regulates artha and kama,
  keeping them from being misused or abused.
- liberation (*moksha*): the highest desire is liberation or Self-

realization. If the first three desires are engaged in with the proper attitude and are in balance, it's easier to turn to spiritual pursuits.

In Buddhism, dharma is often used to refer to cosmic order, natural law, the teachings of the Buddha, codes of conduct, objects, facts, or ideas.

dharmamegha samadhi – from *dharma* = virtue + *megha* = cloud. A state of continuous discernment between the Spirit (Self, Purusha) and Nature (Prakriti). It also includes the complete nonattachment necessary to achieve the highest spiritual rewards. . . Dharmamegha samadhi is the last stage of spiritual development (specifically, the last moments of asamprajnata samadhi) before Self-realization.

dhyana – meditation; the effortless, steady focus of attention on the object of meditation. The seventh of the eight limbs of the Raja Yoga.

diksha – initiation. Central to the tradition of Yoga, it is the entrance into the guru/disciple relationship. Diksha accelerates a student's spiritual potentials through the transmission of shakti (spiritual power) from the teacher to the student.

duhkha –suffering, pain, sorrow, grief. It is not simply a series of unpleasant experiences or the "bad breaks" that are a part of every life. Like viewing a movie slightly out of focus, it is a persistent feeling that something is not right or complete. Due to this lingering discomfort, we never are fully at rest. Duhkha persists even during pleasurable experiences. It continues until we experience the Self.

E

ekagrata – one-pointedness of mind.

ekam – one; Reality. Ekam is used in the well-known phrase from the Rig Veda, *"Ekam sat, vipraha bahudha vadanti," "Truth is one; seers express it in many ways."* This is a central teaching of the nondualistic Advaita Vedanta philosophy, which proclaims that there is one unchanging Absolute Reality, but many paths that lead to realizing It.

G

guna – lit., strand or thread. Quality, attribute, characteristic. One of the three qualities of nature: sattwa, rajas and tamas, or balance, activity, and inertia.

guru – lit., the weighty or venerable one. A spiritual guide. Scriptures such as the *Guru Gita* and the *Advaya-Taraka Upanishad* also state that the syllable, *gu* = darkness and *ru* = remover.

Guru-parampara – any lineage of gurus. In Yoga sutra 1.26, Ishwara is referred to as "*the teacher* (lit., guru) *of even the most ancient teachers* (lit., gurus)."

H

hatha – lit., force. Esoterically, *ha* = sun; *tha* = moon. This refers to the harmonious functioning of opposing energies within the individual. In this, it is much the same as the principles of Yin and Yang. Physiologically, it suggests attaining a proper balance between the sympathetic and parasympathetic nervous systems. See Hatha Yoga, nadi, and prana.

Force suggests that the mind is drawn inward through (the force of) the physical body (as opposed to meditation, which the mind is drawn inward through the will). See Hatha Yoga.

Hatha Yoga – the physical branch of Yoga. It includes postures (*asanas*), breathing techniques (*pranayama*), seals (*mudras*), locks (*bandhas*), deep relaxation (Yoga nidra), and cleansing practices (*kriyas*). Though known for its ability to bring health, flexibility, and relaxation, its ultimate objectives are the purification of the *nadis* (subtle nerve pathways) and uniting of the outgoing and incoming (or upward and downward) flows of prana. When the flow of prana is balanced and harmonious, the mind becomes still and tranquil and ready for the subtler practices of concentration, meditation, and samadhi. Hatha Yoga helps return the body to its state of optimum health and ease.

Hatha Yoga Pradeepika – a classic in the teachings of Hatha Yoga, composed in the fifteenth century by Swami Swatmarama. It is thought to be the oldest text on Hatha Yoga.

I

ida – the *nadi* (subtle nerve current) that flows through the left nostril and the spine. It has a cooling effect on the system as opposed to *pingala*, the heating nadi on the right.

Integral Yoga – the principles and practices of the six major branches of Yoga: Hatha, Jnana, Bhakti, Karma, Japa, and Raja as taught by Sri Swami Satchidananda. The mix and emphasis of the practices is dependent on the taste, natural inclinations, and temperament of the individual.

The great master, Sri Aurobindo, also taught a form of Yoga that he called IntegralYoga.

ishta devata – one's chosen deity. There is only one absolute God with the various deities being manifestations that represent aspects of that one Reality. In Hinduism and Yoga, seekers are free to choose whichever form is most meaningful to them for devotion.

Ishwara – From the verb root *ish* = to rule, to own. Lord, God, the Divine with form, the Supreme Cosmic Soul.

There are several meanings for this term:
- The Supreme ruler and controller; both transcendent and immanent.
- According to Advaita Vedanta, Ishwara is the Absolute (Brahman) as seen from, and limited by, ignorance or illusion.
- The material and efficient cause of the world.
- According to Patanjali: Ishwara is the Supreme Purusha (Self), unaffected by afflictions, karmas, or desires; the omniscient teacher of all teachers; and who expresses through the mantra OM.

Ishwara pranidhanam – worship of God or self-surrender. In the *Yoga Sutras*, it is a means to samadhi, one of the principles of kriya yoga, and one of the niyamas.

J

japa – repetition or recitation, usually of a mantra or name of God.

Japa Yoga – science of mantra repetition. The repetition could be out loud, with lip movement only, mentally, or as writing meditation (*likhit japa*).

jivatman – individual soul. According to Sankhya philosophy, *jivas* (souls) are infinite in number, conscious and eternal. There is neither birth nor death for the jiva. According to Advaita Vedanta, the jiva is a blending of the Self and non-Self due to an incorrect identification of the Self with the body-mind. In Advaita Vedanta, jivas are considered essentially one, although in daily experience, they are perceived as many.

jivanmukta – a liberated living being. Liberation results from the discrimination between the Spirit and Nature – the ultimate dissolution of ignorance (*avidya*).

jnanam (from the root *jna* = to know) – wisdom of the Self; knowledge, idea. The word is often used to refer to insights gained from meditation and samadhi.

Jnana Yoga – Yoga of Self-inquiry, knowledge, and study. Characterized by contemplation on the true nature of the Self, the constant effort to discriminate between what is real (permanent and unchanging) and what is unreal (that which changes).

K

kaivalya – From *kevala* = alone, one. Absolute freedom, independence, isolation, liberation. In the *Yoga Sutras*, it is a term for the enlightened state.

karma – the universal law of action and reaction; cause and effect. Ignorance sustains the law of karma. If mistakenly think that we are the body and mind, our actions cannot help but be influenced by ignorance. We forget that we are peace personified. Our attachments serve to "magnetize" the mind so that we face the consequences of our self-interested expectation.

Once ignorance is transcended, we no longer generate new karmas. Look at sutra 2.12, which states that the womb of karmas has its roots in the klesas (obstacles), which are rooted in ignorance.

Karma is of four classes according to the effects the actions produced.
- white = happiness
- black = unhappiness
- black & white (mixed) = a mix of happiness and sorrow
- neither black nor white = actions – like those of the yogi – which transcend karma, leaving the individual free

Karma can also be classified as follows:
- *Sanjita* – all the accumulated actions from previous births awaiting another lifetime to bear fruit.
- *Prarabdha* – karmas manifesting in the present birth.
- *Agami* – karmas currently being created.

Karma Yoga – performing actions as selfless service without attachment to the results. The fruits of actions can be dedicated to God or humanity. Another practice of Karma Yoga is to experience oneself as only a channel for God's work. There is no sense of being the doer.

karuna – mercy, compassion.

klesa – from *klis* = misery, root obstruction, to be troubled, to suffer distress. Some schools of thought also define klesas as misperception.

koshas – the koshas or sheaths are five coverings that veil the Self. They are, from gross to subtle:
- *anamaya kosha*, physical body
- *pranamaya kosha*, energy body, composed of prana
- *manamaya kosha*, mind
- *vijnanamaya kosha*, wisdom sheath
- *anandaymaya kosha*, sheath composed of bliss

kriya – lit. action, practices. According to the *Yoga Sutras*, it comprises the three preliminary steps in Yoga – tapas, svadhyaya, and Ishwara pranidhanam, or austerity, study, and worship of God or self-surrender. The word is also used to refer to the cleansing practices of Hatha Yoga.

kumbhaka – breath retention. It could be voluntary, as part of the practice of pranayama, or occurring naturally in deep meditative states (in which case it is referred to as *kevala kumbhaka*).

kundalini – lit., coiled energy. The primordial energy stored at the base of the spine in the *muladhara chakra* of every individual. When awakened naturally through a one-pointed mind and the purification of selfishness, it begins to move upward within the subtle central channel (*sushumna*) of the spine, piercing and enlivening the chakras and initiating a total rejuvenation and spiritual evolution of the individual. Because a forced, premature awakening of this energy can result in undesirable consequences, it is compared to a cobra that must be handled with great care.

L

likhit japa – the practice of writing mantras. It is an aid to developing concentration (dharana).

M

mahat = great (in space, time, quality, or degree). Also a synonym for *buddhi*, the discriminative faculty of the mind. According to Sankhya philosophy, it is the cosmic aspect of the intellect and the first expression of Prakriti. The ego evolves from mahat.

Mahat is also used as a term of respect and reverence for evolved spiritual individuals.

maharishi – great sage. From *maha* = great + *drsh* = to see. Maharishi literally means, great seer, the one who has seen (experienced) spiritual truths.

mahavakya – four great statements from the Upanishads and Veda that summarize their essence. They are all suitable to use as objects of meditation:
- Consciousness is Brahman
- This Self is Brahman
- Thou art That
- I am Brahman

mala beads – aids for mantra repetition. There are 108 beads in the typical string with a 109th tied to a tassel. The number 108 is auspicious, representing infinity, one Truth, and the created universe. The 109th, called the *meru*, represents the Highest. They are used like rosary beads, with the practitioner advancing one bead with each repetition. The right hand is used and held at heart level or above. In advancing the beads, the index finger is not used, since it represents the ego which should be kept out of the practice. The meru is never crossed. Instead, the beads are flipped around and the counting begins again. Mala beads are also worn around the neck as reminders of spiritual virtues and goals. In addition, they absorb the vibrations of the mantra, benefitting the wearer by carrying the peace and clarity of the mantra with them.

manas – from the root *man*, to think. The mind. This term has several variations in meaning according to different schools of thought. Manas emerges from the pure (sattwic) aspect of ego (ahamkara). As such, it receives input from the senses and conveys it to the buddhi.

mantra – from *man* = to think + *tra* = protect. A thought that protects. Mantras are sound formulas used for meditation. A mantra can also be a sacred word or phrase of great spiritual significance and power; scriptural hymns.

maya – illusion, the principle of appearance, the mysterious power of creation. It has several shades of meaning:
- The force or quality that persuades us to misperceive the unreal as real, the temporary as permanent, the painful as pleasurable, the non-Self as the Self, and the unconditioned Absolute as having attributes.
- According to Advaita Vedanta, it is the beginningless cause, which creates the illusory manifestation of the universe. It is not ultimately real and cannot function without Brahman. Maya is how the one Reality can appear as many. Because it is illusory, it has significance only on the relative level.
- Since we can only know the Creator through creation, maya can also be understood as the way the Creator reveals Her/His essence.

mudra – sign, seal, or symbol. In Hatha Yoga, it is a posture, a gesture, or movement of the hands, which holds or directs the prana within and influences the mind. Many deities and saints are depicted with mudras that grant strength, fearlessness, aid, and other blessings.

N

nada – sound. The sound heard within deep meditation; the first vibration out of which all creation manifests. Sound is the first manifestation of Brahman.

nadi – subtle channels of energy flow in the body. There are 72,000 such conduits, the most important being *ida, pingala* and *sushumna*. Ida is associated with the cooling, receptive, parasympathetic nervous system-like functions and with the left nostril. Pingala's activities bring movement, heat, and sympathetic nervous system-like functions and is associated with the right nostril. The *sushumna* is the hollow in the center of the spinal cord and is the channel through which the awakened kundalini energy moves in its journey from chakra to chakra until it reaches the crown of the head (*sahasrara*).

The *Yoga Sutras* only mention *kurma nadi* (tortoise-shaped nadi) whose primary function is to bring stability to the body and mind.

nirbija samadhi – without seed. Nirbija samadhi is the highest spiritual state since both conscious thought and samskaras (subconscious or seed impressions) are transcended and complete realization of unity with the Self is attained.

nirodha – From the verb root *rudh* = to obstruct, restrict, arrest, avert + *ni* = down or into. Stilling, restraint, cessation. It refers to the process of stilling all activities of the mind which obscure the experience of the Self. It is applied on four levels: *vritti, pratyaya, samskara* and *sarva*. These four levels describe increasingly deeper attainments of nirodha.
- Vrittis – modifications of the mind-stuff; movements or currents of thought; conceptions, thought processes.
- Pratyaya – notions, beliefs, single thoughts; the thoughts that immediately arise in the mind when it is stimulated by an object.
- Samskara – subconscious impressions.
- Sarva – a complete cessation of all mental activity.

nirvana – to blow out or extinguish. In Buddhist teachings, it refers to the state of liberation. It has also been referred to as unborn, unconditional, unchanging, indescribable, a state of nonattachment to being and non-being; the state of absolute freedom.

nirvichara – samadhi that is beyond insight.

nirvikalpa – a term used in Vedanta for the samadhi that is without thought or imagination. It is analogous to asamprajnata samadhi in the *Yoga Sutras*.

nirvitarka – samadhi that is beyond examination.

niyama – observances that are essential for spiritual seekers. The second of the eight limbs of Yoga. It consists of purity, contentment, accepting pain as a help for purification, and devotion to God.

O

OM – the cosmic sound vibration, which is the source of, and includes, all other sounds and vibrations. OM is the absolute Brahman as sound and the foundation of all mantras. It is composed of the letters A, U, and M, which represent creation, evolution and dissolution, or waking, dreaming, and dreamless sleep. Beyond these states is a fourth, the *anahata* or unrepeated.

P

pada – a one-fourth portion. Each of the four sections of the *Yoga Sutras* is referred to as a pada.

EXPLORE MORE: SANSKRIT GLOSSARY

param – highest, supreme.

Patanjali – the sage who compiled the *Yoga Sutras*. He is often referred to as the "Father of Yoga." Some identify him as also the author of the *Mahabhashya*, an important Sanskrit grammar text, which dates to the second century B.C.E. There are also other works attributed to an author(s) named Patanjali, including texts on medicine. They may or may not be the same person.

In popular tradition, Patanjali is considered an incarnation of the mythical serpent *Ananta* (or *Sesha*), on whom Lord Vishnu rests before the beginning of a new cycle of creation. Symbolically, snakes were said to be the guardians of esoteric teachings and *Ananta*, as Lord of the snakes, presided over them all. *Ananta* took human form as Patanjali to bring Yoga to humanity.

In another version, Patanjali is said to have fallen from the sky as a newborn serpent into the hands of his mother as she was offering water in worship of the sun. She called him Patanjali from *pata* (meaning both serpent and fallen) and *anjali* (referring to hands cupped in worship).

pingala – one of the three main nadis. As with the ida nadi, its opposite and complementary "partner," it originates at the base of the spine. It is associated with the right nostril and has a heating effect.

Prakriti – primordial Nature. In Sankhya philosophy it is one of the two fundamental categories of existence, the other being Purusha (Spirit, consciousness). Although Prakriti is active, consciousness is not intrinsic to its nature. In Advaita Vedanta, Prakriti is a principle of illusion (maya) and is therefore not real.

prana – the vital energy, life breath, life force. Though one, prana is divided into five major categories according to its functions:
- *prana*: rising upwards.
- *apana*: moving downwards. Governs the abdomen and excretory functions.
- *vyana*: governs circulation of blood.
- *samana*: the force that equalizes; also responsible for the digestive process.
- *udana*: directs vital currents upwards.

pranava – OM, life-giver. The basic hum of the vibration of the universe. It is an expression of prana.

pranayama – the practice of regulating the vital force through control of the breath. The fourth of the eight limbs of Raja Yoga.

pranidhanam – to put first. Total dedication, self-surrender. In Buddhism, pranidhanam is taken to mean a vow and usually refers to the Boddisattva's vow of helping all beings attain liberation.

prasadam – consecrated food offering, grace, tranquility.

pratipaksha bhavanam – practice of substituting positive thoughts for disturbing, negative ones. A key practice in Raja Yoga for perfecting moral and ethical virtues and for returning the attention to the object of meditation when it has wandered.

pratyahara – sense control; withdrawal of the senses from their objects (the fifth of the eight limbs of the *Yoga Sutras*). It refers to the proper use of the senses and is the stage that leads to concentration (dharana).

pratyaya – in the context of the *Yoga Sutras*, pratyaya generally refers to the thought that instantly arises when the mind is impacted by an object of perception.

Pratyayas form the content of vrittis, conceptions. While vritti refers to a fundamental mental process or a concept composed of thoughts, pratyaya refers to the content of individual consciousness, which includes the insights (prajna) attained in the lower states of samadhi, which are not the result of vritti activity.

In Sankhya philosophy pratyaya is equivalent to the intellect or buddhi.

puja – worship service

Purusha – the divine Self in all beings; individual soul. Depending on the context, texts might use "Purusha" to refer to the individual soul or to the Absolute God. In Sankhya philosophy, Purusha along with Prakriti constitute the two basic categories of creation. Purusha is pure consciousness, which is unchanging, eternal, and pure. The *Yoga Sutras* also use the word "Seer" and "Owner" to refer to the same reality. According to Advaita Vedanta, Purusha is One and is the eternal witness of all there is.

R

raga – attachment, liking, desire, craving. In the *Yoga Sutras*, attachment is defined as that which follows pleasurable (not necessarily beneficial) experiences. An attachment is anything outside of the Self that we believe we need to be happy. Since anything other than the Self changes (often taking our pleasure with it), attachments are seen as the active cause of our suffering.

raja – king.

Raja Yoga – lit., Royal Yoga. Another name by which the *Yoga Sutras of Patanjali* are known.

rajas – activity; restlessness (one of the three gunas).

S

sananda samadhi – samadhi with ananda (bliss) in which the sattwic mind is experienced.

sasmita samadhi – samadhi in which the ego alone is experienced.

sabda – sound, word, or name.

sabija – with seed. Any experience that leaves seeds of attachments in its wake. These seeds can sprout when activated by external stimulation.

sadhana – leading straight to a goal, guiding well, effective, productive. Refers to spiritual practices and to the cultivation of mindfulness and proper attitudes in life.

sahasrara chakra – the thousand-petaled lotus; the seventh chakra (center of Cosmic consciousness) at the crown of the head. The final resting place of the kundalini energy.

In Saivite traditions (devotees of Lord Siva), it is regarded as Siva's seat within the individual. The kundalini energy is Siva's consort, the goddess Shakti. When she is awakened through sincere sadhana, she travels up through the spine, supercharging the chakras. Reaching the crown chakra, Shakti (representing all force and matter) reunites with her beloved Siva (representing pure consciousness). Their union results in enlightenment for the individual.

shakti, Shakti – energy, power, capacity, the kundalini force; the divine cosmic energy which creates, evolves, and dissolves the universe. As a proper name, *Shakti* is used to designate the consort of Lord Siva or the Divine Mother in general.

samadhi – from *dha* = to hold + *sam* = together completely. Contemplation, superconscious state, absorption. The final limb of the eight limbs listed in the *Yoga Sutras*. Any of several states in which the mind is (to a greater or lesser degree) absorbed in a state of union with the object of meditation. It is beyond thought, untouched by speech or words. It is the experience of unwavering stillness and awareness and leads to intuitive wisdom.

samprajnata samadhi – the state of meditative absorption in which information or understanding regarding the object of meditation is gained intuitively.

samsara – the continuing rounds of birth, death, and rebirth.

samskara – latent, subconscious impression; innate tendency due to past actions.

samyama – the combined practice of dharana, dhyana, and samadhi upon one object. **samyoga** – connection, contact, perfect union.

sangha – a community of like-minded individuals; the disciples of a master.

sankalpa – a resolve or vow.

Sankhya – lit., discrimination, number, enumeration. The philosophical school which identifies the categories of existence. This school of thought teaches a dual reality with two eternal components: Consciousness (Purusha) and primordial matter (Prakriti).

The path involves careful discrimination between Purusha and Prakriti and the rejection of everything but Purusha as the principle of consciousness.

sannyas – renunciation, monkhood. Renouncing worldly possessions and ties. While in formal monkhood, renunciation includes physically giving up personal possessions and family life, its essence, to renounce selfishness, is necessary for anyone who wishes to experience Self-realization.

sat – existence or Truth.

Satchidananda, Swami (1914 - 2002) world-renowned Yoga Master and founder-spiritual head of the Integral Yoga Institutes and Satchidananda Ashrams. He is the inspiration behind the building of the LOTUS (Light Of Truth Universal Shrine). Located at Satchidananda Ashram-Yogaville in Buckingham, Virginia, the LOTUS is a sanctuary dedicated to the One Truth that illumines all faiths.

satsang – lit., keeping company with the truth. Satsang includes group activities centered on the study of spiritual teachings through discourses, group practice, or other activities.

sattwa – purity, balanced state (one of the three gunas).

satya – truth; truthfulness (one of the principles of yama).

savichara samadhi – samadhi with insight

savitarka samadhi – samadhi with examination.

shanti – peace

Sivananda, Swami (1887-1963) – great sage of the Himalayas, founder of the Divine Life Society; author of over three hundred books on Yoga and spiritual life, guru of Sri Swami Satchidananda and many other respected Yoga teachers.

shraddha – faith. From *su* = bright, pure, clean + *hrd* = heart + *dha* = to hold. To hold or rest in a pure heart (a heart filled with light or wisdom). From the roots of the word, we can see that it is more than just belief. It is our natural state and is experienced in a pure, unselfish heart. See *faith* in the English Glossary.

Sri – eminent or illustrious. A prefix placed before names of scriptures and great women and men to show respect or reverence; a name of the Goddess of Wealth.

sutra – lit., thread. Aphorism.

svadhyaya – from *sva* = self + the verb root *adhi* = to go over. Study, scriptural study, study of the self and the Self. One of the niyamas and one of the three practices of Patanjali's kriya yoga (sutra 2.1).

swami – in the Hindu tradition, a renunciate or monk; a member of the Holy Order of Sannyas.

T

tamas – inertia, dullness. One of the three gunas.

tanmatra – subtle essence, energy, or potential that gives rise to material elements. According to Sankhya philosophy, they evolve from the tamasic aspect of the ego principle. The five elements derived from the tanmatras are as follows:
- sound – ether
- touch – air

- sight – fire
- taste – water
- smell – earth

Tantra Yoga – (*Tantra*, from *tan* = do in detail + *tra* = to protect). Tantra is not limited to one school of thought, so it is difficult to generalize about it. We can say that it usually centers on practices using rituals, yantras, and mantras to experience the union of Siva and Shakti (the masculine and feminine or positive and negative forces) within the individual. Some schools lay great emphasis on the chakras and the kundalini energy. Others strive for both enjoyment *and* liberation (this may have been a reaction to the glorification of formal renunciation that was prevalent then). Yoga does not preach a joyless life, but use of the senses in a way that brings happiness, that doesn't simply drain energy, and that advances one toward their spiritual goal.

The divine feminine power is central to most forms of tantra. One school of tantra, which has given it a bad name, involves the ritual use of alcoholic drinks and ritualistic sexual intercourse (not necessarily with one's partner). The use of alcohol may be due to a misinterpretation of *soma*, the nectar of immortality, which is secreted by the pineal gland in deep meditative states. The use of intercourse as a spiritual practice could be a misguided attempt at facilitating the inner union of masculine and feminine.

It should be noted that sexual relations are not forbidden or frowned upon in Yoga. It is perfectly fine for non-monastics to indulge. It's best when it is an expression of love within a loving, caring, committed partnership.

tapas – lit., to burn. Spiritual austerity, purificatory action, accepting but not causing pain. In the *Yoga Sutras*, it is one of the niyamas and one of the three practices in kriya yoga (sutra 2.1).

tattwa – lit., thatness. Category, truth, principle, teachings, the essence of things.

tradak – the meditation practice of gazing at an object.

turiya – lit., the fourth. In the philosophy of Vedanta, it refers to the state that transcends the states of waking, dreaming, and dreamless sleep. It is the eternal, unchanging state of witness consciousness.

U

Upanishads – lit., to devotedly sit close. The final portion of each of the Vedas, which teaches the principles of the nondualistic Advaita Vedanta philosophy. The essential teaching of the Upanishads is that the Self of an individual is the same as Brahman, the Absolute. Therefore, the goal of spiritual life is presented as the realization of Brahman as one's True Identity or Self.

There are ten principle Upanishads: Isha, Kena, Katha, Prasna, Mundaka, Mandukya, Taittiriya, Aitareya, Chandogya, and Brihadaranyaka.

V

vairagya – lit., without color. Dispassion, nonattachment. In the *Yoga Sutras* and the *Bhagavad Gita*, nonattachment, along with practice, is presented as the way to achieve mastery over the mind.

Vedanta – the culmination or end objective of knowledge.

Vedas – the primary revealed wisdom scriptures of Hinduism (Rig, Sama, Yajur, and Atharva).

vidya – knowledge, learning.

viveka – discriminative discernment. Discrimination between the Real and the unreal, the permanent and impermanent, and the Self and the non-Self. A state of ever-present discrimination between that which changes and that which does not. The *Yoga Sutras* teach that by the practice of the limbs of Yoga (see ashtanga Yoga), one develops viveka (2.28) and transcends ignorance.

vritti (from *vrt* = to turn, revolve, roll, move) – modification or fluctuation of the mind-stuff in which the mind seeks to find meaning by linking related pieces of information. According to Advaita Vedanta, vritti activity serves as the connecting link between knower (subject) and known (object) and is what makes knowledge of things within creation possible.

Vyasa (arranger or compiler) – the name of several great sages of Hinduism. His commentary on the *Yoga Sutras* is the oldest in existence, dating from the fifth century, C.E. He is also said to have compiled the four *Vedas*, the *Mahabharata*, the *Bhagavad Gita*, and the *Puranas*. Though tradition has it that the same Vyasa compiled all these scriptures, it is not likely due to the large span of years involved. One reason for this could be that Vyasa is a title rather than a name.

vyutthana – externalization of individual consciousness. It is the predominant characteristic of ordinary consciousness. Vyutthana implies the desire to know the nature of sense objects, believing that they are separate from the self. It also suggests the desire for gaining satisfaction or permanent happiness from the knowledge of those objects. It is mentioned in the *Yoga Sutras* (3.9) as an opposite to nirodha.

yama – abstinence (the first of the eight limbs of Raja Yoga). It includes harmlessness, truthfulness, nonstealing, continence, and nongreed.

Yoga – lit., union. The term has many meanings. Among them: union of the individual with the Absolute, any effort that makes for such union, and a tranquil and clear state of mind under all conditions.

ENGLISH GLOSSARY

attention – prolonged awareness directed toward a thought, object, or image.

Cosmic Consciousness – unlimited, unbounded, omnipresent, omniscient awareness. See Brahman and mahavakya in the *Sanskrit Glossary*.

enlightenment – the state of experiencing the Self as one's True Nature and as the essence of all life and objects in the universe. Also known as Self-realization and God-realization among other terms. In Buddhism it is known as nirvana, in Christianity, mystic union.

faith – (*shraddha*) can have several shades of meaning. Typically, it refers to a religious tradition, to agreeing to a particular set of spiritual teachings, or to belief in things unseen.

Faith can be either conditional or unconditional. Conditional faith is the first stage. It is entering into a working, experimental relationship with a principle or practice that we regard as logical and that holds the promise of bearing the desired fruit. When that principle is verified by direct experience, we attain unconditional faith. Unconditional faith is not a strongly held belief, but a state of certainty based on experience. We have faith – we know – that honey is sweet, not because we were told it is, or that is says so in a cookbook or science text, but because we have verified it by tasting it ourselves.

In sutra 1.20, faith is given as one of the means to experience samadhi.

See *shraddha* in the *Sanskrit Glossary*, and Faith tradition, below.

faith tradition – a term that is sometimes used in place of religion. Too often religion is a loaded term with meanings that obscure the essence of spirituality. To many, a religion is a set of principles that one must agree with and live up to (some principles may be more institutional than scriptural). This mindset is often based on literal interpretations of scripture (which is where everyone starts), and causes some fundamentalists to consider that only their way is correct, while others are fully or partially wrong – even evil.

Use of the term faith tradition, helps us understand the two major facets of religions. The foremost is faith. The content of faith is the esoteric truths that have been directly experienced by the founders or prophets of a tradition and verified by the direct experiences of seekers. Faith is common to all religions.

The second aspect of religions is their traditions. This includes the many customs, events, ceremonies, rituals, myths, and practices of a people who are guided by a sacred text or texts, a prophet, or divine (or divinely inspired) being. An example of a tradition is the time set aside for communal worship. For Christians, worship is on Sundays; for Jews, Fridays. Because spiritual growth can be developed with either practice, we can see that the days mandated for worship may be essential to the tradition, but not for growth in faith. The common truth behind both traditions is that faith can be cultivated by worship, regardless of what day it is observed.

In essence, the term *faith tradition* can help us shift our focus from what divides us to the universal human and spiritual level.

Agnostics and atheists also have faith, maybe not in a Supreme Being, but in science, friendship, logic, or on moral and ethical behavior. They too are looking for peace.

See *faith*, above.

fervor – intensity, enthusiasm. It is an intense wish to achieve or attain an object or state. In meditation, we use the word to mean the motivation that is the result of recognizing the benefits of meditation. In Advaita Vedanta, it is called *mumukshutva* and is one of the qualifications needed for spiritual growth.

Golden Moment – the period just before turning the awareness to the object of meditation near the beginning of a meditation session, and again at the end before closing. It helps create the nonjudgmental attitude needed for success in meditation.

guided meditation – often used for group meditations, it is a step-by-step technique in which various images, thoughts, visualizations, or affirmations are suggested by a group leader during the sitting.

ignorance – the state of being unaware of one's True Nature. See *avidya* in the *Sanskrit Glossary*.

EXPLORE MORE: ENGLISH GLOSSARY

initiation – the transmission of knowledge and empowerment that are part of the process of entering into the guru/disciple relationship. See *diksha* in the *Sanskrit Glossary*.

insight – *prajna* in Sanskrit. Wisdom; intuitive knowledge. In a spiritual context, it is knowledge gained without the means of reason, but through higher mental processes like samadhi. It is not having a "feeling" or sense about a truth, but a direct intuitive encounter with it. It is much like revelation (a revealed truth) in Christian tradition.

intention – directed inspiration. Intention mobilizes physical, psychological, and spiritual energy toward a goal. It is the fuel for regularity and the backdrop for every meditation session.

meditation – the practice of stilling the restless activity of the mind to experience deeper levels of being and inner peace.

mindfulness – the state of remaining acutely aware of all aspects of life around us, and our actions and reactions to events in life.

mindscape – the conscious content of the mind at any moment. It's what we "see" when we take a peek at our awareness.

Nature – one of two principle aspects of creation (consciousness being the other), Nature is the material aspect. See *Prakriti* in the *Sanskrit Glossary*.

nonattachment – the mental state of absence of selfish expectations or desires. An objective, clear state of mind. See *vairagya* in the *Sanskrit Glossary*.

nonjudgmental attitude – the attitude necessary to create the best inner environment for meditation to flourish. It is based on not assessing typical mental activity or content as good or bad. It is also the cultivation of a kind and compassionate attitude toward oneself.

self – the individual self as opposed to the transcendent Self (atman or Purusha).

Self – in Sanskrit, atman or Purusha. Self refers to our True Nature. It is called 'true' because it is unborn, undying, and omnipresent. It is pure unbounded consciousness.

Self-realization – see *enlightenment*.

Spirit – one of two principle aspects of creation, Spirit is the principle of awareness. In Sanskrit, it can be called Purusha, atman, or Brahman.

subtle body – the exact meaning can vary, but it usually refers to the energy body, the second of the five Koshas. See, *koshas* is the Sanskrit glossary.

True Nature – the essence and ground of being. See *Self*.

EXPLORE MORE

FOR FURTHER STUDY

Meditation

To Know Your Self, Swami Satchidananda, Integral Yoga Publications, 2008.

Concentration and Meditation, Swami Sivananda, The Divine Life Society, 1975.

Mind, Its Mysteries & Control, Swami Sivananda, The Divine Life Society, 1997.

Moment of Christ, John Main, OSB, Darton, Longman and Todd, 1984.

Meditation & Its Practices, Swami Adiswarananda, Skylight Paths Publishing, 2003.

Mindfulness: The Path to the Deathless, Venerable Ajahn Sumedho, Amaravati Publications, 1987.

Sacred Texts

The Living Gita, Swami Satchidananda, Integral Yoga Publications, 1988.

Bhagavad Gita: The Beloved Lord's Secret Love Song, Graham M. Schweig, Harper SanFrancisco, 2007.

The Upanishads, Eknath Easwaran, Nilgiri Press, 1995.

The Upanishads, Swami Prabhavananda: The Breath of the Eternal, Vedanta Press, 1971.

Yoga Sutras of Patanjali, Swami Satchidananda, Integral Yoga Publications, 2003.

Hatha Yoga Pradipika, Swami Muktibodhananda, Yoga Publications Trust, 2006.

Inside the Yoga Sutras, Reverend Jaganath Carrera, Integral Yoga Publications, 2010.

Raja Yoga, Swami Vivekananda, Bharatiya Kala Prakashan, 2009.

Branches of Yoga
Integral Yoga Hatha, Swami Satchidananda, Integral Yoga Publications, 1970.

Japa Yoga, Swami Sivananda, The Divine Life Society, 1972.

Jnana Yoga, Swami Vivekananda, Ramakrishna Vivekanada Center, 1982.

Karma Yoga and Bhakti Yoga, Swami Vivekananda, Ramakrishna Vivekanada Center, 1982.

Yoga & Ayurveda, David Frawley, Lotus Press, 1999.

REVEREND JAGANATH CARRERA

Reverend Jaganath is the founder and spiritual head of the Yoga Life Society and author of *Inside the Yoga Sutras: A Comprehensive Sourcebook for the Study and Practice of Patanjali's Yoga Sutras*. He is a direct disciple of world renowned Yoga master and leader in the interfaith movement, Sri Swami Satchidananda, founder of the Integral Yoga Institutes and Satchidananda Ashrams worldwide.

Reverend Jaganath has been teaching all facets of Yoga since 1973 at universities, prisons, Yoga centers, and interfaith programs both here and abroad. He was a principle instructor of both Hatha and Raja Yoga for the Integral Yoga Teacher Training Certification Programs for over twenty years and co-wrote the training manual used for that course. He established the Integral Yoga Ministry and co-developed the highly regarded Integral Yoga Meditation and Raja Yoga Teacher Training Certification programs.

He served for eight years as chief administrator of Satchidananda Ashram-Yogaville and founded the Integral Yoga Institute of New Brunswick, NJ. Reverend Jaganath taught Hatha and Raja Yoga at Rutgers University where he was also a member of the Board of Campus Ministers for eleven years.

Reverend Jaganath holds a Masters Degree in Acupuncture. He served as clinic supervisor, instructor, and Dean of Academics at the Eastern School of Acupuncture, where he also helped develop its highly regarded curriculum.

A master bodyworker, he is certified in medical massage and Reflexology and is proficient in meridian massage and Therapeutic Touch.

Contact Reverend Jaganath

Find information on Reverend Jaganath's teaching schedule as well as informative articles, audios, and videos on all aspects of Yoga on the Yoga Life Society website, www.yogalifesociety.com

You can contact Reverend Jaganath at officeofsriguruji@yogalifesociety.com

ABOUT THE YOGA LIFE SOCIETY AND YOGA LIFE PUBLICATIONS

The Yoga Life Society began in 2005 in response to requests from students of Reverend Jaganath Carrera who were looking to deepen their understanding and experience of Yoga. Since then, people of all faiths and backgrounds have come together to study, practice, support each other, and to serve others in the name of Yoga.

Reverend Jaganath's insightful teachings bring a fresh perspective to the timeless teachings of Yoga while remaining true to its heart: the practical, joyful, and beneficial. His emphasis is on individual and universal peace, lovingkindness, service to all, and a simple, step-by-step approach to spiritual growth. This spirit permeates all the programs, retreats, trainings, and publications offered by the Yoga Life Society.

The Goals of Yoga Life Society include:
- Leading a life of harmony, service, peace, and joy through the study and practice of the six major branches of Yoga: Hatha, Karma, Bhakti, Jnana, Japa, and Raja.
- To create an environment – within and without – in which spiritual ignorance evaporates leading to the experience of Self-realization.
- Bringing lovingkindness and compassion to all.
- Realizing that there is one universal Truth or Reality, and that all faith traditions are valid and complete ways to experience that Truth.

You can visit the Yoga Life Society on facebook and twitter, and at www.yogalifesociety.com.

Yoga Life Publications

Yoga Life Publications exists to disseminate the teachings of Reverend Jaganath through books, booklets, CDs, and DVDs. For more information, visit: www.yogalifesociety.com.

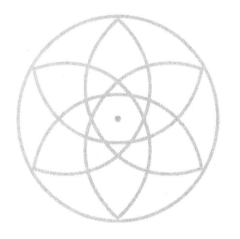